Andrew Lang

A Collection of Ballads

Andrew Lang

A Collection of Ballads

ISBN/EAN: 9783743306257

Manufactured in Europe, USA, Canada, Australia, Japa

Cover: Foto ©ninafisch / pixelio.de

Manufactured and distributed by brebook publishing software (www.brebook.com)

Andrew Lang

A Collection of Ballads

CONTENTS

	PAGE
INTRODUCTION	ix
SIR PATRICK SPENS	1
BATTLE OF OTTERBOURNE	5
TAM LIN	10
THOMAS THE RHYMER	16
SIR HUGH; OR, THE JEW'S DAUGHTER	19
SON DAVIE! SON DAVIE!	22
THE WIFE OF USHER'S WELL	24
THE TWA CORBIES	26
THE BONNIE EARL MORAY	27
CLERK SAUNDERS	30
WALY, WALY	35
LOVE GREGOR; OR, THE LASS OF LOCH-ROYAN	37
THE QUEEN'S MARIE	41
KINMONT WILLIE	45
JAMIE TELFER	52
THE DOUGLAS TRAGEDY ...	59
THE BONNY HIND	62
YOUNG BICHAM	65
LOVING BALLAD OF LORD BATEMAN	69

Contents

	PAGE
THE BONNIE HOUSE O' AIRLY	73
ROB ROY	75
THE BATTLE OF KILLIECRANKIE	77
ANNAN WATER	79
THE ELPHIN NOURRICE	81
COSPATRICK	82
JOHNNIE ARMSTRANG	87
EDOM O' GORDON	92
LADY ANNE BOTHWELL'S LAMENT	98
JOCK O THE SIDE	101
LORD THOMAS AND FAIR ANNET	107
FAIR ANNIE	111
THE DOWIE DENS OF YARROW	116
SIR ROLAND	119
ROSE THE RED AND WHITE LILY	123
THE BATTLE OF HARLAW:	
Evergreen Version	131
Traditionary Version	138
DICKIE MACPHALION	142
A LYKE-WAKE DIRGE	143
THE LAIRD OF WARISTOUN	145
MAY COLVEN	147
JOHNIE FAA	150
HOBBIE NOBLE	152
THE TWA SISTERS	157
MARY AMBREE	160

Contents

	PAGE
ALISON GROSS	165
THE HEIR OF LYNNE	167
GORDON OF BRACKLEY	172
EDWARD, EDWARD	175
YOUNG BENJIE	177
AULD MAITLAND	180
THE BROOMFIELD HILL	189
WILLIE'S LADYE	193
ROBIN HOOD AND THE MONK	196
ROBIN HOOD AND THE POTTER	209
ROBIN HOOD AND THE BUTCHER	221
NOTES	227

INTRODUCTION

WHEN the learned first gave serious attention to popular ballads, from the time of Percy to that of Scott, they laboured under certain disabilities. The Comparative Method was scarcely understood, and was little practised. Editors were content to study the ballads of their own countryside, or, at most, of Great Britain. Teutonic and Northern parallels to our ballads were then adduced, as by Scott and Jamieson. It was later that the ballads of Europe, from the Faroes to Modern Greece, were compared with our own, with European *Märchen*, or children's tales, and with the popular songs, dances, and traditions of classical and savage peoples. The results of this more recent comparison may be briefly stated. Poetry begins, as Aristotle says, in improvisation. Every man is his own poet, and, in moments of stronge motion, expresses himself in song. A typical example is the Song of Lamech in Genesis—

"I have slain a man to my wounding,
And a young man to my hurt."

Instances perpetually occur in the Sagas: Grettir, Egil, Skarphedin, are always singing. In *Kidnapped*, Mr. Stevenson introduces "The Song of the Sword of Alan," a fine example of Celtic practice: words and air are beaten out together, in the heat of victory. In the same way, the women sang improvised dirges, like Helen; lullabies, like the lullaby of Danæ in Simonides, and flower songs, as in modern Italy. Every function of life, war, agriculture, the chase, had its appropriate magical and mimetic dance and song, as in Finland, among Red Indians, and among Australian blacks. "The deeds of men" were chanted by heroes, as by Achilles; stories were told in alternate verse and prose; girls, like Homer's Nausicaa, accompanied dance and ball play, priests and medicine-men accompanied rites and magical ceremonies by songs.

These practices are world-wide, and world-old. The thoroughly popular songs, thus evolved, became the rude material of a professional class of minstrels, when these arose, as in the heroic age of Greece. A minstrel might be attached to a Court, or a noble; or he might go wandering with song and harp among the people. In either case, this class of men developed more regular and ample measures. They evolved the hexameter; the *laisse* of the *Chansons de Geste;* the strange technicalities of Scandinavian poetry; the metres of Vedic hymns; the choral odes of Greece. The narrative popular chant became in their hands the Epic, or the mediæval rhymed romance. The metre of improvised verse changed into the artistic lyric. These lyric forms were fixed, in many cases, by the art of writing. But poetry did not remain solely in professional and literary hands. The mediæval minstrels and *jongleurs* (who may best be studied in Léon Gautier's Introduction to his *Epopées Françaises*) sang in Court and Camp. The poorer, less regular brethren of the art, harped and played conjuring tricks, in farm and grange, or at street corners. The foreign newer metres took the place of the old alliterative English verse. But unprofessional men and women did not cease to make and sing.

Some writers have decided, among them Mr. Courthope, that our traditional ballads are degraded popular survivals of literary poetry. The plots and situations of some ballads are, indeed, the same as those of some literary mediæval romances. But these plots and situations, in Epic and Romance, are themselves the final literary form of *märchen*, myths and inventions originally *popular*, and still, in certain cases, extant in popular form among races which have not yet evolved, or borrowed, the ampler and more polished and complex *genres* of literature. Thus, when a literary romance and a ballad have the same theme, the ballad may be a popular degradation of the romance; or, it may be the original popular shape of it, still surviving in tradition. A well-known case in prose, is that of the French fairy tales.

Perrault, in 1697, borrowed these from tradition and gave them literary and courtly shape. But *Cendrillon* or *Chaperon Rouge* in the mouth of a French peasant, is apt to be the old traditional version, uncontaminated by the refinements of Perrault, despite Perrault's immense success and circulation. Thus tradition preserves pre-literary forms, even though, on occasion, it may borrow from literature. Peasant poets have been authors of ballads, without being, for all that, professional minstrels. Many such poems survive in our ballad literature.

Introduction

The material of the ballad may be either romantic or historical. The former class is based on one of the primeval invented situations, one of the elements of the *Märchen* in prose. Such tales or myths occur in the stories of savages, in the legends of peasants, are interwoven later with the plot in Epic or Romance, and may also inspire ballads. Popular superstitions, the witch, metamorphosis, the returning ghost, the fairy, all of them survivals of the earliest thought, naturally play a great part. The Historical ballad, on the other hand, has a basis of resounding fact, murder, battle, or fire-raising, but the facts, being derived from popular rumour, are immediately corrupted and distorted, sometimes out of all knowledge. Good examples are the ballads on Darnley's murder and the youth of James VI.

In the romantic class, we may take *Tamlane*. Here the idea of fairies stealing children is thoroughly popular; they also steal young men as lovers, and again, men may win fairy brides, by clinging to them through all transformations. A classical example is the seizure of Thetis by Peleus, and Child quotes a modern Cretan example. The dipping in milk and water,

I may add, has precedent in ancient Egypt (in *The Two Brothers*), and in modern Senegambia. The fairy tax, tithe, or teind, paid to Hell, is illustrated by old trials for witchcraft, in Scotland.[1] Now, in literary forms and romance, as in *Ogier le Danois*, persons are carried away by the Fairy King or Queen. But here the literary romance borrows from popular superstition; the ballad has no need to borrow a familiar fact from literary romance. On the whole subject the curious may consult "The Secret Commonwealth of Elves, Fauns, and Fairies," by the Reverend Robert Kirk of Aberfoyle, himself, according to tradition, a victim of the fairies.

Thus, in *Tamlane*, the whole *donnée* is popular. But the current version, that of Scott, is contaminated, as Scott knew, by incongruous modernisms. Burns's version, from tradition, already localizes the events at Carterhaugh, the junction of Ettrick and Yarrow. But Burns's version does not make the Earl of Murray father of the hero, nor the Earl of March father of the heroine. Roxburgh is the hero's father in Burns's variant, which is more plausible, and the modern verses do not occur. This

[1] See Pitcairn, Case of Alison Pearson, 1586.

ballad apparently owes nothing to literary romance.

In *Mary Hamilton* we have a notable instance of the Historical Ballad. No Marie of Mary Stuart's suffered death for child murder.

She had no Marie Hamilton, no Marie Carmichael among her four Maries, though a lady of the latter name was at her court. But early in the reign a Frenchwoman of the queen's was hanged, with her paramour, an apothecary, for slaying her infant. Knox mentions the fact, which is also recorded in letters from the English ambassador, uncited by Mr. Child. Knox adds that there were ballads against the Maries. Now, in March 1719, a Mary Hamilton, of Scots descent, a maid of honour of Catherine of Russia, was hanged for child murder (*Child*, vi. 383). It has therefore been supposed, first by Charles Kirkpatrick Sharpe long ago, later by Professor Child, and then by Mr. Courthope, that our ballad is of 1719, or later, and deals with the Russian, not the Scotch, tragedy.

To this we may reply (1) that we have no example of such a throwing back of a contemporary event, in ballads. (2) There is a version (*Child*, viii. 507) in which Mary Hamilton's paramour is a "pottinger," or apothecary, as in the real old Scotch affair. (3) The number of variants of a ballad is likely to be proportionate to its antiquity and wide distribution. Now only *Sir Patrick Spens* has so many widely different variants as *Mary Hamilton*. These could hardly have been evolved between 1719 and 1790, when Burns quotes the poem as an old ballad. (4) We have no example of a poem so much in the old ballad manner, for perhaps a hundred and fifty years before 1719. The style first degraded and then expired: compare *Rob Roy* and *Killiecrankie*, in this collection, also the ballads of *Loudoun Hill*, *The Battle of Philiphaugh*, and others much earlier than 1719. New styles of popular poetry on contemporary events as *Sherriffmuir* and *Tranent Brae* had arisen. (5) The extreme historic inaccuracy of *Mary Hamilton* is paralleled by that of all the ballads on real events. The mention of the Pottinger is a trace of real history which has no parallel in the Russian affair, and there is no room, says Professor Child, for the supposition that it was voluntarily inserted by reciter or copyist, to tally with the narrative in Knox's History.

On the other side, we have the name of Mary Hamilton occurring in a tragic event of 1719, but then the name does not uniformly appear in the variants of the ballad. The lady is there spoken of generally as Mary Hamilton, but also as Mary Myle, Lady Maisry, as daughter of the Duke of York (Stuart), as Marie Mild, and so forth. Though she bids sailors carry the tale of her doom, she is not abroad, but in Edinburgh town. Nothing can be less probable than that a Scots popular ballad-maker in 1719, telling the tale of a yesterday's tragedy in Russia, should throw the time back by a hundred and fifty years, should change the scene to Scotland (the heart of the sorrow would be Mary's exile), and, above all, should compose a ballad in a style long obsolete. This is not the method of the popular poet, and such imitations of the old ballad as *Hardyknute* show that literary poets of 1719 had not knowledge or skill enough to mimic the antique manner with any success.

We may, therefore, even in face of Professor Child, regard *Mary Hamilton* as an old example of popular perversion of history in ballad, not as "one of the very latest," and also "one of the very best" of Scottish popular ballads.

Rob Roy shows the same power of perversion. It was not Rob Roy but his sons, Robin Oig (who shot Maclaren at the plough-tail), and James Mohr (alternately the spy, the Jacobite, and the Hanoverian spy once more), who carried off the heiress of Edenbelly. Indeed a kind of added epilogue, in a different measure, proves that a poet was aware of the facts, and wished to correct his predecessor.

Such then are ballads, in relation to legend and history. They are, on the whole, with exceptions, absolutely popular in origin, composed by men of the people for the people, and then diffused among and altered by popular reciters. In England they soon won their way into printed stall copies, and were grievously handled and moralized by the hack editors.

No ballad has a stranger history than *The Loving Ballad of Lord Bateman*, illustrated by the pencils of Cruikshank and Thackeray. Their form is a ludicrous cockney perversion, but it retains the essence. Bateman, a captive of "this Turk," is beloved by the Turk's daughter (a staple incident of old French romance), and by her released. The lady after seven years rejoins Lord Bateman: he has just married a local bride, but "orders another marriage," and sends home his bride "in a coach and three." This incident is stereotyped in the ballads and occurs in an example in the Romaic.[1]

Now Lord Bateman is *Young Bekie* in the Scotch ballads, who becomes *Young Beichan, Young Bichem,* and so forth, and has adventures identical with those of Lord Bateman, though the proud porter in the Scots version is scarcely so prominent and illustrious. As Motherwell saw, Bekie (Beichan, Buchan, Bateman) is really Becket, Gilbert Becket, father of Thomas of Canterbury. Every one has heard how *his* Saracen bride sought him in London. (Robert of Gloucester's *Life and Martyrdom of Thomas Becket*, Percy Society. See Child's Introduction, IV., i. 1861, and Motherwell's *Minstrelsy*, p. xv., 1827.) The legend of the dissolved marriage is from the common stock of ballad lore. Motherwell found an example in the state of *Cantefable,* alternate prose and verse,

[1] Translated in *Ballads and Lyrics of Old France.*—A. L.

like *Aucassin and Nicolette.* Thus the cockney rhyme descends from the twelfth century.

Such are a few of the curiosities of the ballad. The examples selected are chiefly chosen for their romantic charm, and for the spirit of the Border raids which they record. A few notes are added in an appendix. The text is chosen from among the many variants in Child's learned but still unfinished collection, and an effort has been made to choose the copies which contain most poetry with most signs of uncontaminated originality. In a few cases Sir Walter Scott's versions, though confessedly "made up," are preferred. Perhaps the editor may be allowed to say that he does not merely plough with Professor Child's heifer, but has made a study of ballads from his boyhood.

This fact may exempt him, even in the eyes of too patriotic American critics, from "the common blame of a plagiary." Indeed, as Professor Child has not yet published his general theory of the Ballad, the editor does not know whether he agrees with the ideas here set forth.

So far the Editor had written, when news came of Professor Child's regretted death. He had lived to finish, it is said, the vast collection of all known traditional Scottish and English Ballads, with all accessible variants, a work of great labour and research, and a distinguished honour to American scholarship. We are not told, however, that he had written a general study of the topic, with his conclusions as to the evolution and diffusion of the Ballads: as to the influences which directed the selection of certain themes of *Märchen* for poetic treatment, and the processes by which identical ballads were distributed throughout Europe. No one, it is to be feared, is left, in Europe at least, whose knowledge of the subject is so wide and scientific as that of Professor Child. It is to be hoped that some pupil of his may complete the task in his sense, if, indeed, he has eft it unfinished.

BALLADS

SIR PATRICK SPENS

(Border Minstrelsy.)

The king sits in Dunfermline town,
   Drinking the blude-red wine o :
"O whare will I get a skeely skipper
   To sail this new ship of mine o?"

O up and spake an eldern-knight,
   Sat at the king's right knee :
"Sir Patrick Spens is the best sailor
   That ever saild the sea."

Our king has written a braid letter,
   And seald it with his hand,
And sent it to Sir Patrick Spens,
   Was walking on the strand.

"To Noroway, to Noroway,
   To Noroway oer the faem ;
The king's daughter of Noroway,
   'Tis thou maun bring her hame."

The first word that Sir Patrick read,
   Sae loud, loud laughed he ;
The neist word that Sir Patrick read,
   The tear blinded his ee.

"O wha is this has done this deed,
　　And tauld the king o me,
To send us out, at this time of the year,
　　To sail upon the sea?"

"Be it wind, be it weet, be it hail, be it sleet,
　　Our ship must sail the faem;
The king's daughter of Noroway,
　　'Tis we must fetch her hame."

They hoysed their sails on Monenday morn,
　　Wi' a' the speed they may;
They hae landed in Noroway,
　　Upon a Wodensday.

They hadna been a week, a week
　　In Noroway but twae,
When that the lords o Noroway
　　Began aloud to say:

"Ye Scottishmen spend a' our king's goud,
　　And a' our queenis fee."
"Ye lie, ye lie, ye liars loud!
　　Fu' loud I hear ye lie!

"For I brought as much white monie
　　As gane my men and me,
And I brought a half-fou' o' gude red goud,
　　Out o'er the sea wi' me.

"Make ready, make ready, my merry-men a'!
　　Our gude ship sails the morn."
"Now ever alake, my master dear,
　　I fear a deadly storm!

"I saw the new moon, late yestreen,
　　Wi' the auld moon in her arm;
And if we gang to sea, master,
　　I fear we'll come to harm."

They hadna sail'd a league, a league,
    A league but barely three,
When the lift grew dark, and the wind blew
    loud,
    And gurly grew the sea.

The ankers brak, and the top-masts lap,
    It was sic a deadly storm;
And the waves cam o'er the broken ship,
    Till a' her sides were torn.

"O where will I get a gude sailor,
    To take my helm in hand,
Till I get up to the tall top-mast,
    To see if I can spy land?"

"O here am I, a sailor gude,
    To take the helm in hand,
Till you go up to the tall top-mast;
    But I fear you'll ne'er spy land."

He hadna gane a step, a step,
    A step but barely ane,
When a bout flew out of our goodly ship,
    And the salt sea it came in.

"Gae, fetch a web o' the silken claith,
    Another o' the twine,
And wap them into our ship's side,
    And let na the sea come in."

They fetchd a web o the silken claith,
    Another o the twine,
And they wapped them roun that gude
    ship's side
    But still the sea came in.

O laith, laith, were our gude Scots lords
    To weet their cork-heel'd shoon!
But lang or a the play was play'd
    They wat their hats aboon,

And mony was the feather-bed
    That fluttered on the faem,
And mony was the gude lord's son
    That never mair cam hame.

The ladyes wrang their fingers white,
    The maidens tore their hair,
A' for the sake of their true loves,
    For them they'll see na mair.

O lang, lang may the ladyes sit,
    Wi' their fans into their hand,
Before they see Sir Patrick Spens
    Come sailing to the strand!

And lang, lang may the maidens sit,
    Wi' their goud kaims in their hair,
A' waiting for their ain dear loves!
    For them they'll see na mair.

O forty miles off Aberdeen,
    'Tis fifty fathoms deep,
And there lies gude Sir Patrick Spens,
    Wi' the Scots lords at his feet.

BATTLE OF OTTERBOURNE
(*Child*, vol. vi.)

It fell about the Lammas tide,
    When the muir-men win their hay,
The doughty Douglas bound him to ride
    Into England, to drive a prey.

He chose the Gordons and the Graemes,
    With them the Lindesays, light and gay;
But the Jardines wald not with him ride,
    And they rue it to this day.

And he has burn'd the dales of Tyne,
    And part of Bambrough shire:
And three good towers on Reidswire fells,
    He left them all on fire.

And he march'd up to Newcastle,
    And rode it round about:
"O wha's the lord of this castle?
    Or wha's the lady o't?"

But up spake proud Lord Percy then,
    And O but he spake hie!
"I am the lord of this castle,
    My wife's the lady gaye."

"If thou'rt the lord of this castle,
    Sae weel it pleases me!
For, ere I cross the Border fells,
    The tane of us sall die."

He took a lang spear in his hand,
   Shod with the metal free,
And for to meet the Douglas there,
   He rode right furiouslie.

But O how pale his lady look'd,
   Frae aff the castle wa',
When down, before the Scottish spear,
   She saw proud Percy fa'.

"Had we twa been upon the green,
   And never an eye to see,
I wad hae had you, flesh and fell;
   But your sword sall gae wi' mee."

"But gae ye up to Otterbourne,
   And wait there dayis three;
And, if I come not ere three dayis end,
   A fause knight ca' ye me."

"The Otterbourne's a bonnie burn;
   'Tis pleasant there to be;
But there is nought at Otterbourne,
   To feed my men and me.

"The deer rins wild on hill and dale,
   The birds fly wild from tree to tree;
But there is neither bread nor kale,
   To feed my men and me.

"Yet I will stay at Otterbourne,
   Where you shall welcome be;
And, if ye come not at three dayis end,
   A fause lord I'll ca' thee."

"Thither will I come," proud Percy said,
   "By the might of Our Ladye!"—
"There will I bide thee," said the Douglas,
   "My troth I plight to thee."

They lighted high on Otterbourne,
    Upon the bent sae brown;
They lighted high on Otterbourne,
    And threw their pallions down.

And he that had a bonnie boy,
    Sent out his horse to grass,
And he that had not a bonnie boy,
    His ain servant he was.

But up then spake a little page,
    Before the peep of dawn:
"O waken ye, waken ye, my good lord,
    For Percy's hard at hand."

"Ye lie, ye lie, ye liar loud!
    Sae loud I hear ye lie;
For Percy had not men yestreen,
    To dight my men and me.

"But I have dream'd a dreary dream,
    Beyond the Isle of Sky;
I saw a dead man win a fight,
    And I think that man was I."

He belted on his guid braid sword,
    And to the field he ran;
But he forgot the helmet good,
    That should have kept his brain.

When Percy wi the Douglas met,
    I wat he was fu fain!
They swakked their swords, till sair they swat,
    And the blood ran down like rain.

But Percy with his good broad sword,
    That could so sharply wound,
Has wounded Douglas on the brow,
    Till he fell to the ground.

Then he calld on his little foot-page,
    And said—"Run speedilie,
And fetch my ain dear sister's son,
    Sir Hugh Montgomery.

"My nephew good," the Douglas said,
    "What recks the death of ane!
Last night I dreamd a dreary dream,
    And I ken the day's thy ain.

"My wound is deep; I fain would sleep;
    Take thou the vanguard of the three,
And hide me by the braken bush,
    That grows on yonder lilye lee.

"O bury me by the braken-bush,
    Beneath the blooming brier;
Let never living mortal ken
    That ere a kindly Scot lies here."

He lifted up that noble lord,
    Wi the saut tear in his e'e;
He hid him in the braken bush,
    That his merrie men might not see.

The moon was clear, the day drew near,
    The spears in flinders flew,
But mony a gallant Englishman
    Ere day the Scotsmen slew.

The Gordons good, in English blood,
    They steepd their hose and shoon;
The Lindesays flew like fire about,
    Till all the fray was done.

The Percy and Montgomery met,
    That either of other were fain;
They swapped swords, and they twa swat,
    And aye the blood ran down between.

"Yield thee, now yield thee, Percy," he said,
  "Or else I vow I'll lay thee low!"
"To whom must I yield," quoth Earl Percy,
  "Now that I see it must be so?"

"Thou shalt not yield to lord nor loun,
  Nor yet shalt thou yield to me;
But yield thee to the braken-bush,
  That grows upon yon lilye lee!"

"I will not yield to a braken-bush,
  Nor yet will I yield to a brier;
But I would yield to Earl Douglas,
  Or Sir Hugh the Montgomery, if he were here."

As soon as he knew it was Montgomery,
  He stuck his sword's point in the gronde;
The Montgomery was a courteous knight,
  And quickly took him by the honde.

This deed was done at Otterbourne,
  About the breaking of the day;
Earl Douglas was buried at the braken bush,
  And the Percy led captive away.

TAM LIN

(*Child*, Part II., p. 340, Burns's Version.)

O I FORBID you, maidens a',
    That wear gowd on your hair,
To come or gae by Carterhaugh,
    For young Tam Lin is there.

There's nane that gaes by Carterhaugh
    But they leave him a wad,
Either their rings, or green mantles,
    Or else their maidenhead.

Janet has kilted her green kirtle
    A little aboon her knee,
And she has braided her yellow hair
    A little aboon her bree,
And she's awa' to Carterhaugh,
    As fast as she can hie.

When she came to Carterhaugh
    Tam Lin was at the well,
And there she fand his steed standing,
    But away was himsel.

She had na pu'd a double rose,
    A rose but only twa,
Till up then started young Tam Lin,
    Says, " Lady, thou's pu nae mae.

TAM LIN.

p. 10.

"Why pu's thou the rose, Janet,
  And why breaks thou the wand?
Or why comes thou to Carterhaugh
  Withoutten my command?"

"Carterhaugh, it is my ain,
  My daddie gave it me;
I'll come and gang by Carterhaugh,
  And ask nae leave at thee."

 . . . . .

Janet has kilted her green kirtle
  A little aboon her knee,
And she has snooded her yellow hair
  A little aboon her bree,
And she is to her father's ha,
  As fast as she can hie.

Four and twenty ladies fair
  Were playing at the ba,
And out then cam the fair Janet,
  Ance the flower amang them a'.

Four and twenty ladies fair
  Were playing at the chess,
And out then cam the fair Janet,
  As green as onie grass.

Out then spak an auld grey knight,
  Lay oer the castle wa,
And says, "Alas, fair Janet, for thee
  But we'll be blamed a'."

"Haud your tongue, ye auld-fac'd knight,
  Some ill death may ye die!
Father my bairn on whom I will,
  I'll father nane on thee."

Out then spak her father dear,
    And he spak meek and mild;
"And ever alas, sweet Janet," he says,
    "I think thou gaes wi child."

"If that I gae wi' child, father,
    Mysel maun bear the blame;
There's neer a laird about your ha
    Shall get the bairn's name.

"If my love were an earthly knight,
    As he's an elfin grey,
I wad na gie my ain true-love
    For nae lord that ye hae.

"The steed that my true-love rides on
    Is lighter than the wind;
Wi siller he is shod before
    Wi burning gowd behind."

Janet has kilted her green kirtle
    A little aboon her knee,
And she has snooded her yellow hair
    A little aboon her bree,
And she's awa' to Carterhaugh,
    As fast as she can hie.

When she cam to Carterhaugh,
    Tam Lin was at the well,
And there she fand his steed standing,
    But away was himsel.

She had na pu'd a double rose,
    A rose but only twa,
Till up then started young Tam Lin,
    Says, "Lady, thou pu's nae mae.

"Why pu's thou the rose, Janet,
    Amang the groves sae green,
And a' to kill the bonie babe
    That we gat us between?"

"O tell me, tell me, Tam Lin," she says,
  "For's sake that died on tree,
If eer ye was in holy chapel,
  Or christendom did see?"

"Roxbrugh he was my grandfather,
  Took me with him to bide,
And ance it fell upon a day
  That wae did me betide.

"And ance it fell upon a day,
  A cauld day and a snell,
When we were frae the hunting come,
  That frae my horse I fell;
The Queen o Fairies she caught me,
  In yon green hill to dwell.

"And pleasant is the fairy land,
  But, an eerie tale to tell,
Ay at the end of seven years
  We pay a tiend to hell;
I am sae fair and fu' o flesh
  I'm feared it be mysel.

"But the night is Halloween, lady,
  The morn is Hallowday;
Then win me, win me, an ye will,
  For weel I wat ye may.

"Just at the mirk and midnight hour
  The fairy folk will ride,
And they that wad their true-love win,
  At Miles Cross they maun bide."

"But how shall I thee ken, Tam Lin,
  Or how my true-love know,
Amang sae mony unco knights
  The like I never saw?"

"O first let pass the black, lady,
    And syne let pass the brown,
But quickly run to the milk-white steed,
    Pu ye his rider down.

"For I'll ride on the milk-white steed,
    And ay nearest the town;
Because I was an earthly knight
    They gie me that renown.

"My right hand will be glovd, lady,
    My left hand will be bare,
Cockt up shall my bonnet be,
    And kaimd down shall my hair;
And thae's the takens I gie thee,
    Nae doubt I will be there.

"They'll turn me in your arms, lady,
    Into an esk and adder;
But hold me fast, and fear me not,
    I am your bairn's father.

"They'll turn me to a bear sae grim,
    And then a lion bold;
But hold me fast, and fear me not,
    As ye shall love your child.

"Again they'll turn me in your arms
    To a red het gaud of airn;
But hold me fast, and fear me not,
    I'll do to you nae harm.

"And last they'll turn me in your arms
    Into the burning gleed;
Then throw me into well water,
    O throw me in wi speed.

"And then I'll be your ain true-love,
    I'll turn a naked knight;
Then cover me wi your green mantle,
    And cover me out o sight."

Gloomy, gloomy was the night,
  And eerie was the way,
As fair Jenny in her green mantle
  To Miles Cross she did gae.

About the middle o' the night
  She heard the bridles ring;
This lady was as glad at that
  As any earthly thing.

First she let the black pass by,
  And syne she let the brown;
But quickly she ran to the milk-white steed,
  And pu'd the rider down.

Sae weel she minded whae he did say,
  And young Tam Lin did win;
Syne coverd him wi her green mantle,
  As blythe's a bird in spring.

Out then spak the Queen o Fairies,
  Out of a bush o broom:
"Them that has gotten young Tam Lin
  Has gotten a stately groom."

Out then spak the Queen o Fairies,
  And an angry woman was she;
"Shame betide her ill-far'd face,
  And an ill death may she die,
For she's taen awa the bonniest knight
  In a' my companie.

"But had I kend, Tam Lin," she says,
  "What now this night I see,
I wad hae taen out thy twa grey e'en,
  And put in twa een o tree."

THOMAS THE RHYMER
(*Child*, Part II., p. 317.)

True Thomas lay on Huntlie bank;
    A ferlie he spied wi' his ee;
And there he saw a lady bright,
    Come riding down by the Eildon Tree.

Her skirt was o the grass-green silk,
    Her mantle o the velvet fyne, .
At ilka tett of her horse's mane
    Hang fifty siller bells and nine.

True Thomas he pulld aff his cap,
    And louted low down to his knee:
"All hail, thou mighty Queen of Heaven!
    For thy peer on earth I never did see.

"O no, O no, Thomas," she said,
    "That name does not belang to me;
I am but the queen of fair Elfland,
    That am hither come to visit thee.

"Harp and carp, Thomas," she said,
    "Harp and carp, along wi' me,
And if ye dare to kiss my lips,
    Sure of your bodie I will be!"

"Betide me weal, betide me woe,
    That weird sall never daunton me;'
Syne he has kissed her rosy lips,
    All underneath the Eildon Tree.

"Now, ye maun go wi me," she said,
 "True Thomas, ye maun go wi me,
And ye maun serve me seven years,
 Thro weal or woe as may chance to be."

She mounted on her milk-white steed,
 She's taen True Thomas up behind,
And aye wheneer her bridle rung,
 The steed flew swifter than the wind.

O they rade on, and farther on—
 The steed gaed swifter than the wind—
Until they reached a desart wide,
 And living land was left behind.

"Light down, light down, now, True Thomas,
 And lean your head upon my knee;
Abide and rest a little space,
 And I will shew you ferlies three.

"O see ye not yon narrow road,
 So thick beset with thorns and briers?
That is the path of righteousness,
 Tho after it but few enquires.

"And see ye not that braid braid road,
 That lies across that lily leven?
That is the path of wickedness,
 Tho some call it the road to heaven.

"And see not ye that bonny road,
 That winds about the fernie brae?
That is the road to fair Elfland,
 Where thou and I this night maun gae.

"But, Thomas, ye maun hold your tongue,
 Whatever ye may hear or see,
For, if you speak word in Elflyn land,
 Ye'll neer get back to your ain countrie."

O they rade on, and farther on,
  And they waded thro rivers aboon the knee,
And they saw neither sun nor moon,
  But they heard the roaring of the sea.

It was mirk mirk night, and there was nae stern light,
  And they waded thro red blude to the knee ;
For a' the blude that's shed on earth
  Rins thro the springs o that countrie.

Syne they came on to a garden green,
  And she pu'd an apple frae a tree :
" Take this for thy wages, True Thomas,
  It will give the tongue that can never lie."

" My tongue is mine ain," True Thomas said,
  " A gudely gift ye wad gie to me !
I neither dought to buy nor sell,
  At fair or tryst where I may be.

" I dought neither speak to prince or peer,
  Nor ask of grace from fair ladye : "
" Now hold thy peace," the lady said,
  " For as I say, so must it be."

He has gotten a coat of the even cloth,
  And a pair of shoes of velvet green,
And till seven years were gane and past
  True Thomas on earth was never seen.

"SIR HUGH; OR THE JEW'S DAUGHTER"

(*Child*, vol. v.)

FOUR-AND-TWENTY bonny boys
  Were playing at the ba,
And by it came him sweet Sir Hugh,
  And he playd o'er them a'.

He kickd the ba with his right foot
  And catchd it wi his knee,
And throuch-and-thro the Jew's window
  He gard the bonny ba flee.

He's doen him to the Jew's castell
  And walkd it round about;
And there he saw the Jew's daughter,
  At the window looking out.

"Throw down the ba, ye Jew's daughter,
  Throw down the ba to me!"
"Never a bit," says the Jew's daughter,
  "Till up to me come ye."

"How will I come up? How can I come up?
  How can I come to thee?
For as ye did to my auld father,
  The same ye'll do to me."

She's gane till her father's garden,
  And pu'd an apple red and green;
'Twas a' to wyle him sweet Sir Hugh,
  And to entice him in.

She's led him in through ae dark door,
    And sae has she thro nine;
She's laid him on a dressing-table,
    And stickit him like a swine.

And first came out the thick, thick blood,
    And syne came out the thin;
And syne came out the bonny heart's blood;
    There was nae mair within.

She's rowd him in a cake o lead,
    Bade him lie still and sleep;
She's thrown him in Our Lady's draw-well,
    Was fifty fathom deep.

When bells were rung, and mass was sung,
    And a' the bairns came hame,
When every lady gat hame her son,
    The Lady Maisry gat nane.

She's taen her mantle her about,
    Her coffer by the hand,
And she's gane out to seek her son,
    And wanderd o'er the land.

She's doen her to the Jew's castell,
    Where a' were fast asleep:
"Gin ye be there, my sweet Sir Hugh,
    I pray you to me speak."

"Gae hame, gae hame, my mither dear,
    Prepare my winding-sheet,
And at the back o merry Lincoln
    The morn I will you meet."

Now Lady Maisry is gane hame,
    Make him a winding-sheet,
And at the back o merry Lincoln,
    The dead corpse did her meet.

And a the bells o merry Lincoln
   Without men's hands were rung,
And a' the books o merry Lincoln
   Were read without man's tongue,
And neer was such a burial
   Sin Adam's days begun.

SON DAVIE! SON DAVIE!

(*Mackay.*)

"What bluid's that on thy coat lap?
   Son Davie! Son Davie!
What bluid's that on thy coat lap?
   And the truth come tell to me, O."

"It is the bluid of my great hawk,
   Mother lady, Mother lady!
It is the bluid of my great hawk,
   And the truth I hae tald to thee, O."

"Hawk's bluid was ne'er sae red,
   Son Davie! Son Davie!
Hawk's bluid was ne'er sae red,
   And the truth come tell to me, O."

"It is the bluid of my grey hound,
   Mother lady! Mother lady!
It is the bluid of my grey hound,
   And it wudna rin for me, O."

"Hound's bluid was ne'er sae red,
   Son Davie! Son Davie!
Hound's bluid was ne'er sae red,
   And the truth come tell to me, O."

"It is the bluid o' my brother John,
   Mother lady! Mother lady!
It is the bluid o' my brother John,
   And the truth I hae tald to thee, O."

"What about did the plea begin?
  Son Davie! Son Davie!"
"It began about the cutting o' a willow
    wand,
  That would never hae been a tree, O."

"What death dost thou desire to die?
  Son Davie! Son Davie!
What death dost thou desire to die?
  And the truth come tell to me, O."

"I'll set my foot in a bottomless ship,
  Mother lady! mother lady!
I'll set my foot in a bottomless ship,
  And ye'll never see mair o' me, O."

"What wilt thou leave to thy **poor wife?**
  Son Davie! Son Davie!"
"Grief and sorrow all her life,
  And she'll never get mair frae me, O."

"What wilt thou leave to thy young son?
  Son Davie! son Davie!"
"The weary warld to wander up and down,
  And he'll never get mair o' me, O."

"What wilt thou leave to thy mother dear?
  Son Davie! Son Davie!"
"A fire o' coals to burn her wi' hearty
    cheer,
  And she'll never get mair o' me, O."

THE WIFE OF USHER'S WELL

(*Child*, vol. iii.)

There lived a wife at Usher's Well,
    And a wealthy wife was she;
She had three stout and stalwart sons,
    And sent them oer the sea,

They hadna been a week from her,
    A week but barely ane,
When word came to the carline wife
    That her three sons were gane.

They hadna been a week from her,
    A week but barely three,
Whan word came to the carlin wife
    That her sons she'd never see.

" I wish the wind may never cease,
    Nor fashes in the flood,
Till my three sons come hame to me,
    In earthly flesh and blood ! "

It fell about the Martinmass,
    Whan nights are lang and mirk,
The carline wife's three sons came hame,
    And their hats were o the birk.

It neither grew in syke nor ditch,
    Nor yet in ony sheugh ;
But at the gates o Paradise
    That birk grew fair eneugh.

.   .   .   .   .

"Blow up the fire, my maidens!
  Bring water from the well;
For a' my house shall feast this night,
  Since my three sons are well."

And she has made to them a bed,
  She's made it large and wide;
And she's taen her mantle her about,
  Sat down at the bedside.

.   .   .   .   .

Up then crew the red, red cock,
  And up and crew the gray;
The eldest to the youngest said,
  "'Tis time we were away."

The cock he hadna crawd but once,
  And clapp'd his wings at a',
Whan the youngest to the eldest said,
  "Brother, we must awa.

"The cock doth craw, the day doth daw,
  The channerin worm doth chide;
Gin we be mist out o our place,
  A sair pain we maun bide.

"Fare ye weel, my mother dear!
  Fareweel to barn and byre!
And fare ye weel, the bonny lass
  That kindles my mother's fire!"

THE TWA CORBIES

(*Child*, vol. i.)

As I was walking all alane,
I heard twa corbies making a mane;
The tane unto the t'other say,
"Where sall we gang and dine the day?"

"In behint yon auld fail dyke,
I wot there lies a new-slain knight;
And naebody kens that he lies there
But his hawk, his hound, and his lady fair.

"His hound is to the hunting gane,
His hawk to fetch the wild-fowl hame,
His lady's ta'en another mate,
So we may make our dinner sweet.

"Ye'll sit on his white hause-bane,
And I'll pike out his bonny blue een;
Wi ae lock o his gowden hair
We'll theek our nest when it grows bare.

"Mony a one for him makes mane,
But nane sall ken whae he is gane,
Oer his white banes, when they are bare,
The wind sall blaw for evermair."

THE BONNIE EARL MORAY
(*Child*, vol. vi.)
A.

Ye Highlands, and ye Lawlands
   Oh where have you been?
They have slain the Earl of Murray,
   And they layd him on the green.

"Now wae be to thee, Huntly!
   And wherefore did you sae?
I bade you bring him wi you,
   But forbade you him to slay."

He was a braw gallant,
   And he rid at the ring;
And the bonny Earl of Murray,
   Oh he might have been a King!

He was a braw gallant,
   And he playd at the ba;
And the bonny Earl of Murray,
   Was the flower amang them a'.

He was a braw gallant,
   And he playd at the glove;
And the bonny Earl of Murray,
   Oh he was the Queen's love!

Oh lang will his lady
   Look oer the castle Down,
Eer she see the Earl of Murray
   Come sounding thro the town!
     Eer she, etc.

B.

"Open the gates
and let him come in;
  He is my brother Huntly,
he'll do him nae harm."

The gates they were opent,
  they let him come in,
But fause traitor Huntly,
  he did him great harm.

He's ben and ben,
  and ben to his bed,
And with a sharp rapier
  he stabbed him dead.

The lady came down the stair,
  wringing her hands:
"He has slain the Earl o Murray,
  the flower o Scotland."

But Huntly lap on his horse,
  rade to the King:
"Ye're welcome hame, Huntly,
  and whare hae ye been?

"Where hae ye been?
  and how hae ye sped?"
"I've killed the Earl o Murray
  dead in his bed."

"Foul fa you, Huntly!
  and why did ye so?
You might have taen the Earl o Murray,
  and saved his life too."

"Her bread it's to bake,
   her yill is to brew ;
My sister's a widow,
   and sair do I rue.

"Her corn grows ripe,
   her meadows grow green,
But in bonnie Dinnibristle
   I darena be seen."

CLERK SAUNDERS

(*Child*, vol. iii.)

Clerk Saunders and may Margaret
   Walked ower yon garden green;
And sad and heavy was the love
   That fell thir twa between.

"A bed, a bed," Clerk Saunders said,
   "A bed for you and me!"
"Fye na, fye na," said may Margaret,
   "Till anes we married be.

"For in may come my seven bauld brothers,
   Wi' torches burning bright;
They'll say,—'We hae but ae sister,
   And behold she's wi a knight!'"

"Then take the sword frae my scabbard,
   And slowly lift the pin;
And you may swear, and save your aith,
   Ye never let Clerk Saunders in.

"And take a napkin in your hand,
   And tie up baith your bonny e'en,
And you may swear, and save your aith,
   Ye saw me na since late yestreen."

It was about the midnight hour,
   When they asleep were laid,
When in and came her seven brothers,
   Wi' torches burning red.

When in and came her seven brothers,
   Wi' torches burning bright :
They said, "We hae but ae sister,
   And behold her lying with a knight !"

Then out and spake the first o' them,
   " I bear the sword shall gar him die !"
And out and spake the second o' them,
   " His father has nae mair than he !"

And out and spake the third o' them,
   " I wot that they are lovers dear !"
And out and spake the fourth o' them,
   " They hae been in love this mony a year !"

Then out and spake the fifth o' them,
   " It were great sin true love to twain !"
And out and spake the sixth o' them,
   " It were shame to slay a sleeping man !"

Then up and gat the seventh o' them,
   And never a word spake he ;
But he has striped his bright brown brand
   Out through Clerk Saunders' fair bodye.

Clark Saunders he started, and Margaret she turned
   Into his arms as asleep she lay ;
And sad and silent was the night
   That was atween thir twae.

And they lay still and sleeped sound
   Until the day began to daw ;
And kindly to him she did say,
   " It is time, true love, you were awa'."

But he lay still, and sleeped sound,
   Albeit the sun began to sheen;
She looked atween her and the wa',
   And dull and drowsie were his e'en.

Then in and came her father dear;
  Said,—" Let a' your mourning be:
I'll carry the dead corpse to the clay,
  And I'll come back and comfort thee."

" Comfort weel your seven sons;
  For comforted will I never be:
I ween 'twas neither knave nor loon
  Was in the bower last night wi' me.

The clinking bell gaed through the town,
  To carry the dead corse to the clay;
And Clerk Saunders stood at may Margaret's
    window,
  I wot, an hour before the day.

" Are ye sleeping, Margaret?" he says,
  " Or are ye waking presentlie?
Give me my faith and troth again,
  I wot, true love, I gied to thee."

" Your faith and troth ye sall never get,
  Nor our true love sall never twin,
Until ye come within my bower,
  And kiss me cheik and chin."

" My mouth it is full cold, Margaret,
  It has the smell, now, of the ground;
And if I kiss thy comely mouth,
  Thy days of life will not be lang.

" O, cocks are crowing a merry midnight
  I wot the wild fowls are boding day;
Give me my faith and troth again,
  And let me fare me on my way."

" Thy faith and troth thou sall na get,
  And our true love sall never twin,
Until ye tell what comes of women,
  I wot, who die in strong traivelling?

"Their beds are made in the heavens high,
  Down at the foot of our good lord's knee,
Weel set about wi' gillyflowers;
  I wot, sweet company for to see.

"O, cocks are crowing a merry midnight,
  I wot the wild fowl are boding day;
The psalms of heaven will soon be sung,
  And I, ere now, will be missed away."

Then she has ta'en a crystal wand,
  And she has stroken her troth thereon;
She has given it him out at the shot-window,
  Wi' mony a sad sigh, and heavy groan.

"I thank ye, Marg'ret, I thank ye, Marg'ret;
  And aye I thank ye heartilie;
Gin ever the dead come for the quick,
  Be sure, Marg'ret, I'll come for thee."

It's hosen and shoon, and gown alone,
  She climb'd the wall, and followed him,
Until she came to the green forest,
  And there she lost the sight o' him.

"Is there ony room at your head, Saunders?
  Is there ony room at your feet?
Is there ony room at your side, Saunders,
  Where fain, fain I wad sleep?"

"There's nae room at my head, Marg'ret,
  There's nae room at my feet;
My bed it is full lowly now,
  Amang the hungry worms I sleep.

"Cauld mould is my covering now,
  But and my winding-sheet;
The dew it falls nae sooner down
  Than my resting-place is weet.

"But plait a wand o' bonnie birk,
   And lay it on my breast;
And shed a tear upon my grave,
   And wish my saul gude rest.

"And fair Marg'ret, and rare Marg'ret,
   And Marg'ret, o' veritie,
Gin ere ye love another man,
   Ne'er love him as ye did me."

Then up and crew the milk-white cock,
   And up and crew the gray :
Her lover vanish'd in the air,
   And she gaed weeping away.

WALY, WALY

(Mackay.)

O WALY, waly, up the bank,
    O waly, waly, down the brae.
And waly, waly, yon burn side,
    Where I and my love wont to gae.
I leaned my back unto an aik,
    An' thocht it was a trustie tree,
But first it bow'd and syne it brak,
    Sae my true love did lichtly me.

O waly, waly, but love is bonnie
    A little time while it is new,
But when it's auld it waxes cauld,
    And fades away like morning dew.
O wherefore should I busk my head,
    O wherefore should I kame my hair,
For my true love has me forsook,
    And says he'll never love me mair.

Now Arthur's Seat shall be my bed,
    The sheets shall ne'er be pressed by me,
St. Anton's well shall be my drink,
    Since my true love has forsaken me.
Martinmas wind, when wilt thou blaw,
    And shake the green leaves off the tree!
O gentle Death, when wilt thou come?
    For of my life I am wearie!

"Tis not the frost that freezes fell,
   Nor blawing snaw's inclemencie,
'Tis not sic cauld that makes me cry,
   But my love's heart's grown cauld to me.
When we came in by Glasgow toun
   We were a comely sicht to see;
My love was clad in the black velvet,
   And I mysel in cramasie.

But had I wist before I kist
   That love had been sae ill to win,
I'd locked my heart in a case of gold,
   And pinned it wi' a siller pin.
Oh, oh! if my young babe were born,
   And set upon the nurse's knee;
And I myself were dead and gane,
   And the green grass growing over me!

LOVE GREGOR; OR, THE LASS OF LOCHROYAN

(Child, Part III., p. 220.)

"O WHA will shoe my fu' fair foot?
   And wha will glove my hand?
And wha will lace my middle jimp,
   Wi' the new-made London band?

"And wha will kaim my yellow hair,
   Wi' the new made silver kaim?
And wha will father my young son,
   Till Love Gregor come hame?"

"Your father will shoe your fu' fair foot,
   Your mother will glove your hand;
Your sister will lace your middle jimp
   Wi' the new-made London band.

"Your brother will kaim your yellow hair,
   Wi' the new made silver kaim;
And the king of heaven will father your bairn,
   Till Love Gregor come haim."

"But I will get a bonny boat,
   And I will sail the sea,
For I maun gang to Love Gregor,
   Since he canno come hame to me."

O she has gotten a bonny boat,
   And sailld the sa't sea fame;
She langd to see her ain true-love,
   Since he could no come hame.

"O row your boat, my mariners,
  And bring me to the land,
For yonder I see my love's castle,
  Close by the sa't sea strand."

She has ta'en her young son in her arms,
  And to the door she's gone,
And lang she's knocked and sair she ca'd,
  But answer got she none.

"O open the door, Love Gregor," she says,
  "O open, and let me in;
For the wind blaws thro' my yellow hair,
  And the rain draps o'er my chin."

"Awa, awa, ye ill woman,
  You'r nae come here for good;
You'r but some witch, or wile warlock,
  Or mer-maid of the flood."

"I am neither a witch nor a wile warlock,
  Nor mer-maid of the sea,
I am Fair Annie of Rough Royal;
  O open the door to me."

"Gin ye be Annie of Rough Royal—
  And I trust ye are not she—
Now tell me some of the love-tokens
  That past between you and me."

"O dinna you mind now, Love Gregor,
  When we sat at the wine,
How we changed the rings frae our fingers?
  And I can show thee thine.

"O yours was good, and good enough,
  But ay the best was mine;
For yours was o' the good red goud,
  But mine o' the diamonds fine.

"But open the door now, Love Gregor,
   O open the door I pray,
For your young son that is in my arms
   Will be dead ere it be day."

"Awa, awa, ye ill woman,
   For here ye shanno win in;
Gae drown ye in the raging sea,
   Or hang on the gallows-pin."

When the cock had crawn, and day did dawn,
   And the sun began to peep,
Then up he rose him, Love Gregor,
   And sair, sair did he weep.

"O I dreamd a dream, my mother dear,
   The thoughts o' it gars me greet,
That Fair Annie of Rough Royal
   Lay cauld dead at my feet."

"Gin it be for Annie of Rough Royal
   That ye make a' this din,
She stood a' last night at this door,
   But I trow she wan no in."

"O wae betide ye, ill woman,
   An ill dead may ye die!
That ye woudno open the door to her,
   Nor yet woud waken me."

O he has gone down to yon shore-side,
   As fast as he could fare;
He saw Fair Annie in her boat,
   But the wind it tossd her sair.

And "Hey, Annie!" and "How, Annie!
   O Annie, winna ye bide?"
But ay the mair that he cried "Annie,"
   The braider grew the tide.

And "Hey, Annie!" and "How, Annie!
    Dear Annie, speak to me!"
But ay the louder he cried "Annie,"
    The louder roard the sea.

The wind blew loud, the sea grew rough,
    And dashd the boat on shore;
Fair Annie floats on the raging sea,
    But her young son rose no more.

Love Gregor tare his yellow hair,
    And made a heavy moan;
Fair Annie's corpse lay at his feet,
    But his bonny young son was gone.

O cherry, cherry was her cheek,
    And gowden was her hair,
But clay cold were her rosey lips,
    Nae spark of life was there,

And first he's kissd her cherry cheek,
    And neist he's kissed her chin;
And saftly pressd her rosey lips,
    But there was nae breath within.

"O wae betide my cruel mother,
    And an ill dead may she die!
For she turnd my true-love frae my door,
    When she came sae far to me."

THE QUEEN'S MARIE

(Child, vi., *Border Minstrelsy.)*

Marie Hamilton's to the kirk gane,
　Wi ribbons in her hair;
The king thought mair o Marie Hamilton,
　Than ony that were there.

Marie Hamilton's to the kirk gane,
　Wi ribbons on her breast;
The king thought mair o Marie Hamilton,
　Than he listend to the priest.

Marie Hamilton's to the kirk gane,
　Wi gloves upon her hands;
The king thought mair o Marie Hamilton,
　Than the queen and a' her lands.

She hadna been about the king's court
　A month, but barely one,
Till she was beloved by a' the king's court,
　And the king the only man.

She hadna been about the king's court
　A month, but barely three,
Till frae the king's court Marie Hamilton,
　Marie Hamilton durst na be.

The king is to the Abbey gane,
　To pu the Abbey tree,
To scale the babe frae Marie's heart;
　But the thing it wadna be.

O she has rowd it in her apron,
    And set it on the sea :
"Gae sink ye, or swim ye, bonny babe,
    Ye's get na mair o me."

Word is to the kitchen gane,
    And word is to the ha,
And word is to the noble room,
    Amang the ladyes a',
That Marie Hamilton's brought to bed,
    And the bonny babe's mist and awa.

Scarcely had she lain down again,
    And scarcely faen asleep,
When up then started our gude queen,
    Just at her bed-feet,
Saying "Marie Hamilton, where's your babe?
    For I am sure I heard it greet."

"O no, O no, my noble queen !
    Think no such thing to be !
'Twas but a stitch into my side,
    And sair it troubles me."

"Get up, get up, Marie Hamilton,
    Get up, and follow me,
For I am going to Edinburgh town,
    A rich wedding for to see."

O slowly, slowly raise she up,
    And slowly put she on ;
And slowly rode she out the way,
    Wi mony a weary groan.

The queen was clad in scarlet,
    Her merry maids all in green ;
And every town that they cam to,
    They took Marie for the queen.

"Ride hooly, hooly, gentlemen,
　Ride hooly now wi' me!
For never, I am sure, a wearier burd
　Rade in your cumpanie."

But little wist Marie Hamilton,
　When she rade on the brown,
That she was ga'en to Edinburgh town,
　And a' to be put down.

"Why weep ye so, ye burgess-wives,
　Why look ye so on me?
O, I am going to Edinburgh town,
　A rich wedding for to see!"

When she gaed up the Tolbooth stairs,
　The corks frae her heels did flee;
And lang or eer she cam down again,
　She was condemned to die.

When she cam to the Netherbow Port,
　She laughed loud laughters three;
But when she cam to the gallows-foot,
　The tears blinded her ee.

"Yestreen the queen had four Maries,
　The night she'll hae but three;
There was Marie Seaton, and Marie Beaton,
　And Marie Carmichael, and me.

"O, often have I dressd my queen,
　And put gold upon her hair;
But now I've gotten for my reward
　The gallows to be my share.

"Often have I dressd my queen,
　And often made her bed:
But now I've gotten for my reward
　The gallows-tree to tread.

"I charge ye all, ye mariners,
  When ye sail ower the faem,
Let neither my father nor mother get wit,
  But that I'm coming hame.

"I charge ye all, ye mariners,
  That sail upon the sea,
Let neither my father nor mother get wit,
  This dog's death I'm to die.

"For if my father and mother got wit,
  And my bold brethren three,
O mickle wad be the gude red blude,
  This day wad be spilt for me!

"O little did my mother ken,
  The day she cradled me,
The lands I was to travel in,
  Or the death I was to die!"

THE QUEEN'S MARIE.

p. 65.

KINMONT WILLIE

(*Child*, vol. vi.)

O HAVE ye na heard o the fause Sakelde?
　O have ye na heard o the keen Lord
　　Scroop?
How they hae taen bauld Kinmont Willie,
　On Hairibee to hang him up?

Had Willie had but twenty men,
　But twenty men as stout as he,
Fause Sakelde had never the Kinmont taen
　Wi eight score in his companie.

They band his legs beneath the steed,
　They tied his hands behind his back;
They guarded him, fivesome on each side,
　And they brought him ower the Liddel-
　　rack.

They led him thro the Liddel-rack,
　And also thro the Carlisle sands;
They brought him to Carlisle castell,
　To be at my Lord Scroope's commands.

"My hands are tied, but my tongue is free,
　And whae will dare this deed avow?
Or answer by the border law?
　Or answer to the bauld Buccleuch?"

"Now haud thy tongue, thou rank reiver!
　There's never a Scot shall set ye free:
Before ye cross my castle-yate,
　I trow ye shall take farewell o me."

"Fear na ye that, my lord," quo Willie :
 "By the faith o my body, Lord Scroope,"
   he said,
"I never yet lodged in a hostelrie—
 But I paid my lawing before I gaed."

Now word is gane to the bauld Keeper,
 In Branksome Ha where that he lay,
That Lord Scroope has taen the Kinmont
   Willie,
 Between the hours of night and day.

He has taen the table wi his hand,
 He garrd the red wine spring on hie ;
"Now Christ's curse on my head," he said,
 "But avengèd of Lord Scroope I'll be !

"O is my basnet a widow's curch ?
 Or my lance a wand of the willow-tree ?
Or my arm a lady's lilye hand,
 That an English lord should lightly me ?

"And have they taen him, Kinmont Willie,
 Against the truce of Border tide ?
And forgotten that the bauld Bacleuch
 Is keeper here on the Scottish side ?

"And have they een taen him, Kinmont
   Willie,
 Withouten either dread or fear,
And forgotten that the bauld Bacleuch
 Can back a steed, or shake a spear ?

"O were there war between the lands,
 As well I wot that there is none,
I would slight Carlisle castell high,
 Tho it were builded of marble stone.

"I would set that castell in a low,
   And sloken it with English blood;
There's nevir a man in Cumberland
   Should ken where Carlisle castell stood.

"But since nae war's between the lands,
   And there is peace, and peace should be;
I'll neither harm English lad or lass,
   And yet the Kinmont freed shall be!"

He has calld him forty marchmen bauld,
   I trow they were of his ain name,
Except Sir Gilbert Elliot, calld
   The Laird of Stobs, I mean the same.

He has calld him forty marchmen bauld,
   Were kinsmen to the bauld Buccleuch,
With spur on heel, and splent on spauld,
   And gleuves of green, and feathers blue.

There were five and five before them a',
   Wi hunting-horns and bugles bright;
And five and five came wi Buccleuch,
   Like Warden's men, arrayed for fight.

And five and five, like a mason-gang,
   That carried the ladders lang and hie;
And five and five, like broken men;
   And so they reached the Woodhouselee.

And as we crossd the Bateable Land,
   When to the English side we held,
The first o men that we met wi,
   Whae sould it be but fause Sakelde!

"Where be ye gaun, ye hunters keen?"
   Quo fause Sakelde; "come tell to me!"
"We go to hunt an English stag,
   Has trespassed on the Scots countrie."

"Where be ye gaun, ye marshal-men?"
    Quo fause Sakelde; "come tell me true!"
"We go to catch a rank reiver,
    Has broken faith wi the bauld Buccleuch."

"Where are ye gaun, ye mason-lads,
    Wi a' your ladders lang and hie?"
"We gang to herry a corbie's nest,
    That wons not far frae Woodhouselee."

"Where be ye gaun, ye broken men?"
    Quo fause Sakelde; "come tell to me?"
Now Dickie of Dryhope led that band,
    And the nevir a word o lear had he.

"Why trespass ye on the English side?
    Row-footed outlaws, stand!" quo he;
The neer a word had Dickie to say,
    Sae he thrust the lance thro his fause bodie.

Then on we held for Carlisle toun,
    And at Staneshaw-bank the Eden we crossd;
The water was great and meikle of spait,
    But the nevir a horse nor man we lost.

And when we reachd the Staneshaw-bank,
    The wind was rising loud and hie;
And there the laird garrd leave our steeds,
    For fear that they should stamp and nie.

And when we left the Staneshaw-bank,
    The wind began full loud to blaw;
But 'twas wind and weet, and fire and sleet,
    When we came beneath the castell-wa.

We crept on knees, and held our breath,
    Till we placed the ladders against the wa;
And sae ready was Buccleuch himsell
    To mount the first, before us a'.

He has taen the watchman by the throat,
    He flung him down upon the lead:
"Had there not been peace between our
      lands,
    Upon the other side thou hadst gaed."

"Now sound out, trumpets!" quo Buccleuch;
    "Let's waken Lord Scroope right merrilie!"
Then loud the warden's trumpet blew
    "O whae dare meddle wi me?"

Then speedilie to wark we gaed,
    And raised the slogan ane and a',
And cut a hole through a sheet of lead,
    And so we wan to the castel-ha.

They thought King James and a' his men
    Had won the house wi bow and speir;
It was but twenty Scots and ten
    That put a thousand in sic a stear!

Wi coulters, and wi fore-hammers,
    We garrd the bars bang merrilie,
Until we came to the inner prison,
    Where Willie o Kinmont he did lie.

And when we came to the lower prison,
    Where Willie o Kinmont he did lie,
"O sleep ye, wake ye, Kinmont Willie,
    Upon the morn that thou's to die?"

"O I sleep saft, and I wake aft,
    It's lang since sleeping was fley'd frae me;
Gie my service back to my wyfe and bairns
    And a' gude fellows that speer for me."

Then Red Rowan has hente him up,
    The starkest man in Teviotdale:
"Abide, abide now, Red Rowan,
    Till of my Lord Scroope I take farewell.

"Farewell, farewell, my gude Lord Scroope!
 My gude Lord Scroope, farewell!" he cried;
"I'll pay you for my lodging-maill,
 When first we meet on the border-side."

Then shoulder high, with shout and cry,
 We bore him down the ladder lang;
At every stride Red Rowan made,
 I wot the Kinmont's airms playd clang!

"O mony a time," quo Kinmont Willie,
 "I have ridden horse baith wild and wood;
But a rougher beast than Red Rowan,
 I ween my legs have neer bestrode.

"And mony a time," quo Kinmont Willie,
 "I've pricked a horse out oure the furs;
But since the day I backed a steed
 I nevir wore sic cumbrous spurs!"

We scarce had won the Staneshaw-bank,
 When a' the Carlisle bells were rung,
And a thousand men, in horse and foot,
 Cam wi the keen Lord Scroope along.

Buccleuch has turned to Eden Water,
 Even where it flowd frae bank to brim,
And he has plunged in wi a' his band,
 And safely swam them thro the stream.

He turned him on the other side,
 And at Lord Scroope his glove flung he:
"If ye like na my visit in merry England,
 In fair Scotland come visit me!"

All sore astonished stood Lord Scroope,
 He stood as still as rock of stane;
He scarcely dared to trew his eyes,
 When thro the water they had gane.

" He is either himsell a devil frae hell,
　Or else his mother a witch maun be ;
I wad na have ridden that wan water
　For a' the gowd in Christentie."

JAMIE TELFER

(*Child*, vol. vi. Early Edition.)

It fell about the Martinmas tyde,
  When our Border steeds get corn and hay
The captain of Bewcastle hath bound him to ryde,
  And he's ower to Tividale to drive a prey.

The first ae guide that they met wi',
  It was high up Hardhaughswire;
The second guide that we met wi',
  It was laigh down in Borthwick water.

"What tidings, what tidings, my trusty guide?"
  "Nae tidings, nae tidings, I hae to thee;
But, gin ye'll gae to the fair Dodhead,
  Mony a cow's cauf I'll let thee see."

And whan they cam to the fair Dodhead,
  Right hastily they clam the peel;
They loosed the kye out, ane and a',
  And ranshackled the house right weel.

Now Jamie Telfer's heart was sair,
  The tear aye rowing in his e'e;
He pled wi' the captain to hae his gear,
  Or else revenged he wad be.

The captain turned him round and leugh;
  Said—"Man, there's naething in thy house,
But ae auld sword without a sheath,
  That hardly now wad fell a mouse!"

The sun was na up, but the moon was down,
  It was the gryming o' a new fa'n snaw,
Jamie Telfer has run three myles a-foot,
  Between the Dodhead and the Stobs's Ha'

And whan he cam to the fair tower yate,
  He shouted loud, and cried weel hie,
Till out bespak auld Gibby Elliot—
  " Wha's this that brings the fraye to me?"

" It's I, Jamie Telfer o' the fair Dodhead,
  And a harried man I think I be !
There's naething left at the fair Dodhead,
  But a waefu' wife and bairnies three."

" Gae seek your succour at Branksome Ha'.
  For succour ye'se get nane frae me !
Gae seek your succour where ye paid black-
    mail,
  For, man ! ye ne'er paid money to me."

Jamie has turned him round about,
  I wat the tear blinded his e'e—
" I'll ne'er pay mail to Elliot again,
  And the fair Dodhead I'll never see !

" My hounds may a' rin masterless,
  My hawks may fly frae tree to tree ;
My lord may grip my vassal lands,
  For there again maun I never be."

He has turned him to the Tiviot side,
  E'en as fast as he could drie,
Till he came to the Coultart Cleugh
  And there he shouted baith loud and hie.

Then up bespak him auld Jock Grieve—
  " Wha's this that brings the fray to me?"
" It's I, Jamie Telfer o' the fair Dodhead,
  A harried man I trow I be.

" There's naething left in the fair **Dodhead**,
   But a greeting wife and bairnies three,
And sax poor câ's stand in the sta',
   A' routing loud for their minnie."

" Alack a wae ! " quo' auld Jock Grieve,
   " Alack ! my heart is sair for thee !
For I was married on the elder sister,
   And you on the youngest of a' the three."

Then he has ta'en out a bonny black,
   Was right weel fed wi' corn and hay,
And he's set Jamie Telfer on his back,
   To the Catslockhill to tak' the fray.

And whan he cam to the Catslockhill,
   He shouted loud and weel cried he,
Till out and spak him William's Wat—
   " O wha's this brings the fraye to me ? "

" It's I, Jamie Telfer o' the fair Dodhead,
   A harried man I think I be !
The captain of Bewcastle has driven my gear ;
   For God's sake rise, and succour me ! "

" Alas for wae ! " quo' William's Wat,
   " Alack, for thee my heart is sair !
I never cam by the fair Dodhead,
   That ever I fand thy basket bare."

He's set his twa sons on coal-black steeds,
   Himsel' upon a freckled gray,
And they are on wi' Jamie Telfer,
   To Branksome Ha' to tak the fray.

And whan they cam to Branksome Ha',
   They shouted a' baith loud and hie,
Till up and spak him auld Buccleuch,
   Said—" Wha's this brings the fray to me ? "

"It's I, Jame Telfer o' the fair Dodhead,
   And a harried man I think I be!
There's nought left in the fair Dodhead,
   But a greeting wife and bairnies three."

"Alack for wae!" quoth the gude auld lord,
   "And ever my heart is wae for thee!
But fye gar cry on Willie, my son,
   And see that he come to me speedilie!

"Gar warn the water, braid and wide,
   Gar warn it soon and hastily!
They that winna ride for Telfer's kye,
   Let them never look in the face o' me!

"Warn Wat o' Harden, and his sons,
   Wi' them will Borthwick water ride;
Warn Gaudilands, and Allanhaugh,
   And Gilmanscleugh, and Commonside.

"Ride by the gate at Priesthaughswire,
   And warn the Currors o' the Lee;
As ye come down the Hermitage Slack,
   Warn doughty Willie o' Gorrinbery."

The Scots they rade, the Scots they ran,
   Sae starkly and sae steadilie!
And aye the ower-word o' the thrang,
   Was—"Rise for Branksome readilie!"

The gear was driven the Frostylee up,
   Frae the Frostylee unto the plain,
Whan Willie has looked his men before,
   And saw the kye right fast driving.

"Wha drives thir kye?" 'gan Willie say,
   "To mak an outspeckle o' me?"
"It's I, the captain o' Bewcastle, Willie;
   I winna layne my name for thee."

"O will ye let Telfer's kye gae back,
   Or will ye do aught for regard o' me?
Or, by the faith o' my body," quo' Willie Scott,
   "I'se ware my dame's cauf's-skin on thee!"

"I winna let the kye gae back,
   Neither for thy love, nor yet thy fear,
But I will drive Jamie Telfer's kye,
   In spite of every Scot that's here."

"Set on them, lads!" quo' Willie than,
   "Fye, lads, set on them cruellie!
For ere they win to the Ritterford,
   Mony a toom saddle there sall be!"

But Willie was stricken ower the head,
   And through the knapscap the sword has gane;
And Harden grat for very rage,
   Whan Willie on the ground lay slain.

But he's ta'en aff his gude steel-cap,
   And thrice he's waved it in the air—
The Dinlay snaw was ne'er mair white,
   Nor the lyart locks of Harden's hair.

"Revenge! revenge!" auld Wat 'gan cry;
   "Fye, lads, lay on them cruellie!
We'll ne'er see Tiviotside again,
   Or Willie's death revenged shall be."

O mony a horse ran masterless,
   The splintered lances flew on hie;
But or they wan to the Kershope ford,
   The Scots had gotten the victory.

John o' Brigham there was slain,
   And John o' Barlow, as I hear say;
And thirty mae o' the captain's men,
   Lay bleeding on the grund that day.

The captain was run thro' the thick of the
   thigh—
  And broken was his right leg bane;
If he had lived this hundred year,
  He had never been loved by woman again.

" Hae back thy kye ! " the captain said ;
  " Dear kye, I trow, to some they be !
For gin I suld live a hundred years,
  There will ne'er fair lady smile on me."

Then word is gane to the captain's bride,
  Even in the bower where that she lay,
That her lord was prisoner in enemy's land,
  Since into Tividale he had led the way.

" I wad lourd have had a winding-sheet,
  And helped to put it ower his head,
Ere he had been disgraced by the Border Scot,
  When he ower Liddel his men did lead ! "

There was a wild gallant amang us a',
  His name was Watty wi' the Wudspurs,
Cried—" On for his house in Stanegirthside,
  If ony man will ride with us ! "

When they cam to the Stanegirthside,
  They dang wi' trees, and burst the door ;
They loosed out a' the captain's kye,
  And set them forth our lads before.

There was an auld wife ayont the fire,
  A wee bit o' the captain's kin—
" Wha daur loose out the captain's kye,
  Or answer to him and his men ? "

" It's I, Watty Wudspurs, loose the kye,
  I winna layne my name frae thee !
And I will loose out the captain's kye,
  In scorn of a' his men and he."

When they cam to the fair Dodhead,
   They were a wellcum sight to see!
For instead of his ain ten milk-kye,
   Jamie Telfer has gotten thirty and three.

And he has paid the rescue shot,
   Baith wi' goud, and white monie;
And at the burial o' Willie Scott,
   I wot was mony a weeping e'e.

THE DOUGLAS TRAGEDY

(*Child*, vol. ii. Early Edition.)

" Rise up, rise up now, Lord Douglas," she says,
 " And put on your armour so bright ;
Let it never be said, that a daughter of thine
 Was married to a lord under night.

" Rise up, rise up, my seven bold sons,
 And put on your armour so bright,
And take better care of your youngest sister,
 For your eldest's awa the last night."—

He's mounted her on a milk-white steed,
 And himself on a dapple grey,
With a bugelet horn hung down by his side,
 And lightly they rode away.

Lord William lookit o'er his left shoulder,
 To see what he could see,
And there he spy'd her seven brethren bold,
 Come riding o'er the lee.

" Light down, light down, Lady Marg'ret," he said,
 " And hold my steed in your hand,
Until that against your seven brothers bold,
 And your father I make a stand."—

She held his steed in her milk white hand,
 And never shed one tear,
Until that she saw her seven brethren fa',
 And her father hard fighting, who loved her so dear.

"O hold your hand, Lord William!" she said,
  "For your strokes they are wondrous sair;
True lovers I can get many a ane,
  But a father I can never get mair."—

O she's ta'en out her handkerchief,
  It was o' the holland sae fine,
And aye she dighted her father's bloody wounds,
  That were redder than the wine.

"O chuse, O chuse, Lady Marg'ret," he said,
  "O whether will ye gang or bide?"
"I'll gang, I'll gang, Lord William," she said,
  "For ye have left me no other guide."—

He's lifted her on a milk-white steed,
  And himself on a dapple grey.
With a bugelet horn hung down by his side,
  And slowly they baith rade away.

O they rade on, and on they rade,
  And a' by the light of the moon,
Until they came to yon wan water,
  And there they lighted down.

They lighted down to tak a drink
  Of the spring that ran sae clear:
And down the stream ran his gude heart's blood,
  And sair she 'gan to fear.

"Hold up, hold up, Lord William," she says,
  "For I fear that you are slain!"
"'Tis naething but the shadow of my scarlet cloak
  That shines in the water sae plain."

O they rade on, and on they rade,
   And a' by the light of the moon,
Until they cam to his mother's ha' door,
   And there they lighted down.

"Get up, get up, lady mother," he says,
   "Get up, and let me in!—
Get up, get up, lady mother," he says,
   "For this night my fair ladye I've win.

"O mak my bed, lady mother," he says,
   "O mak it braid and deep!
And lay Lady Marg'ret close at my back,
   And the sounder I will sleep."—

Lord William was dead lang ere midnight,
   Lady Marg'ret lang ere day—
And all true lovers that go thegither,
   May they have mair luck than they!

Lord William was buried in St. Marie's kirk,
   Lady Margaret in Marie's quire;
Out o' the lady's grave grew a bonny red rose,
   And out o' the knight's a brier.

And they twa met, and they twa plat,
   And fain they wad be near;
And a' the warld might ken right weel,
   They were twa lovers dear.

But by and rade the Black Douglas,
   And wow but he was rough!
For he pull'd up the bonny brier,
   An flang't in St. Marie's Loch.

THE BONNY HIND

(*Child*, vol. ii.)

O MAY she comes, and may she goes,
  Down by yon gardens green,
And there she spied a gallant squire
  As squire had ever been.

And may she comes, and may she goes,
  Down by yon hollin tree,
And there she spied a brisk young squire,
  And a brisk young squire was he.

" Give me your green manteel, fair maid,
  Give me your maidenhead ;
Gif ye winna gie me your green manteel,
  Gi me your maidenhead."

He has taen her by the milk-white hand,
  And softly laid her down,
And when he's lifted her up again
  Given her a silver kaim.

" Perhaps there may be bairns, kind sir,
  Perhaps there may be nane ;
But if you be a courtier,
  You'll tell to me your name."

" I am na courtier, fair maid,
  But new come frae the sea ;
I am nae courtier, fair maid,
  But when I court 'ith thee.

"They call me Jack when I'm abroad,
    Sometimes they call me John ;
But when I'm in my father's bower
    Jock Randal is my name."

"Ye lee, ye lee, ye bonny lad,
    Sae loud's I hear ye lee !
For I'm Lord Randal's yae daughter,
    He has nae mair nor me."

"Ye lee, ye lee, ye bonny may,
    Sae loud's I hear ye lee !
For I'm Lord Randal's yae yae son,
    Just now come oer the sea."

She's putten her hand down by her spare,
    And out she's taen a knife,
And she has putn't in her heart's bluid,
    And taen away her life.

And he's taen up his bonny sister,
    With the big tear in his een,
And he has buried his bonny sister
    Amang the hollins green.

And syne he's hyed him oer the dale,
    His father dear to see :
"Sing O and O for my bonny hind,
    Beneath yon hollin tree !"

"What needs you care for your bonny hyn ?
    For it you needna care ;
There's aught score hyns in yonder park,
    And five score hyns to spare.

"Fourscore of them are siller-shod,
    Of thae ye may get three ; "
"But O and O for my bonny hyn,
    Beneath yon hollin tree ! "

"What needs you care for your bonny hyn?
   For it you needna care;
Take you the best, gi me the warst,
   Since plenty is to spare."

"I care na for your hyns, my lord,
   I care na for your fee;
But O and O for my bonny hyn,
   Beneath the hollin tree!"

"O were ye at your sister's bower,
   Your sister fair to see,
Ye'll think na mair o your bonny hyn
   Beneath the hollin tree."

  .   .   .   .   .

YOUNG BICHAM

(Child, vol. ii.)

In London city was Bicham born,
    He longd strange countries for to see,
But he was taen by a savage Moor,
    Who handld him right cruely.

For thro his shoulder he put a bore,
    An thro the bore has pitten a tree,
And he's gard him draw the carts o wine,
    Where horse and oxen had wont to be.

He's casten [him] in a dungeon deep,
    Where he coud neither hear nor see;
He's shut him up in a prison strong,
    An he's handld him right cruely.

O this Moor he had but ae daughter,
    I wot her name was Shusy Pye;
She's doen her to the prison-house,
    And she's calld young Bicham one word by.

"O hae ye ony lands or rents,
    Or citys in your ain country,
Coud free you out of prison strong,
    An coud maintain a lady free?"

O London city is my own,
    An other citys twa or three,
Coud loose me out o prison strong,
    An could maintain a lady free."

O she has bribed her father's men
   Wi meikle goud and white money,
She's gotten the key o the prison doors,
   And she has set Young Bicham free.

She's gi'n him a loaf o good white bread,
   But an a flask o Spanish wine,
An she bad him mind on the ladie's love
   That sae kindly freed him out o pine.

"Go set your foot on good ship-board,
   An haste you back to your ain country,
An before that seven years has an end,
   Come back again, love, and marry me."

It was long or seven years had an end
   She longd fu sair her love to see;
She's set her foot on good ship-board,
   An turnd her back on her ain country.

She's saild up, so has she down,
   Till she came to the other side;
She's landed at Young Bicham's gates,
   An I hop this day she sal be his bride.

"Is this Young Bicham's gates?" says she,
   "Or is that noble prince within?"
"He's up the stair wi his bonny bride,
   An monny a lord and lady wi him."

"O has he taen a bonny bride,
   An has he clean forgotten me?"
An sighing said that gay lady,
   "I wish I were in my ain country!"

She's pitten her han in her pocket,
   An gin the porter guineas three;
Says, "Take ye that, ye proud porter,
   An bid the bridegroom speak to me."

O whan the porter came up the stair,
   He's fa'n low down upon his knee:
"Won up, won up, ye proud porter,
   And what makes a' this courtesy?"

"O I've been porter at your gates
   This mair nor seven years an three,
But there is a lady at them now
   The like of whom I never did see.

"For on every finger she has a ring,
   An on the mid-finger she has three,
An there's as meikle goud aboon her brow
   As woud buy an earldom o lan to me."

Then up it started Young Bicham,
   An sware so loud by Our Lady,
"It can be nane but Shusy Pye,
   That has come oor the sea to me."

O quickly ran he down the stair,
   O fifteen steps he has made but three;
He's tane his bonny love in his arms
   An a wot he kissd her tenderly.

"O hae you tane a bonny bride?
   An hae you quite forsaken me?
An hae ye quite forgotten her
   That gae you life an liberty?"

She's lookit oer her left shoulder
   To hide the tears stood in her ee;
"Now fare thee well, Young Bicham," she says,
   "I'll strive to think nae mair on thee."

"Take back your daughter, madam," he says,
　"An a double dowry I'll gie her wi ;
For I maun marry my first true love,
　That's done and suffered so much for me."

He's tak his bonny love by the han,
　And led her to yon fountain stane ;
He's changed her name frae Shusy Pye,
　An he's cald her his bonny love, Lady Jane.

THE LOVING BALLAD OF LORD BATEMAN

(*Child*, vol. ii. Cockney copy.)

LORD BATEMAN was a noble lord,
    A noble lord of high degree;
He shipped himself all aboard of a ship,
    Some foreign country for to see.

He sailed east, he sailed west,
    Until he came to famed Turkey,
Where he was taken and put to prison,
    Until his life was quite weary.

All in this prison there grew a tree,
    O there it grew so stout and strong!
Where he was chained all by the middle,
    Until his life was almost gone.

This Turk he had one only daughter,
    The fairest my two eyes eer see;
She steal the keys of her father's prison,
    And swore Lord Bateman she would let go free.

O she took him to her father's cellar,
    And gave to him the best of wine;
And every health she drank unto him
    Was "I wish, Lord Bateman, as you was mine."

"O have you got houses, have you got land,
   And does Northumberland belong to thee?
And what would you give to the fair young lady
   As out of prison would let you go free?"

"O I've got houses and I've got land,
   And half Northumberland belongs to me;
And I will give it all to the fair young lady
   As out of prison would let me go free."

"O in seven long years I'll make a vow
   For seven long years, and keep it strong,
That if you'll wed no other woman,
   O I will wed no other man."

O she took him to her father's harbor,
   And gave to him a ship of fame,
Saying, "Farewell, farewell to you, Lord Bateman,
   I fear I shall never see you again."

Now seven long years is gone and past,
   And fourteen days, well known to me;
She packed up all her gay clothing,
   And swore Lord Bateman she would go see.

O when she arrived at Lord Bateman's castle,
   How boldly then she rang the bell!
"Who's there? who's there?" cries the proud young porter,
   "O come unto me pray quickly tell."

"O is this here Lord Bateman's castle,
   And is his lordship here within?"
"O yes, O yes," cries the proud young porter,
   "He's just now taking his young bride in."

"O bid him to send me a slice of bread,
  And a bottle of the very best wine,
And not forgetting the fair young lady
  As did release him when close confine."

O away and away went this proud young
    porter,
  O away and away and away went he,
Until he came to Lord Bateman's chamber,
  Where he went down on his bended knee.

"What news, what news, my proud young
    porter?
  What news, what news? come tell to me:"
"O there is the fairest young lady
  As ever my two eyes did see.

"She has got rings on every finger,
  And on one finger she has got three;
With as much gay gold about her middle
  As would buy half Northumberlee.

"O she bids you to send her a slice of bread,
  And a bottle of the very best wine,
And not forgetting the fair young lady
  As did release you when close confine."

Lord Bateman then in passion flew,
  And broke his sword in splinters three,
Saying, "I will give half of my father's land,
  If so be as Sophia has crossed the sea."

Then up and spoke this young bride's mother,
  Who never was heard to speak so free;
Saying, "You'll not forget my only daughter,
  If so be Sophia has crossed the sea."

"O it's true I made a bride of your daughter,
  But she's neither the better nor the worse
    for me;
She came to me with a horse and saddle,
  But she may go home in a coach and
    three."

Lord Bateman then prepared another marriage,
  With both their hearts so full of glee,
Saying, "I will roam no more to foreign
    countries,
  Now that Sophia has crossed the sea."

THE BONNIE HOUSE O' AIRLY

(*Child*, vol. vii. Early Edition.)

It fell on a day, and a bonnie summer day,
  When the corn grew green and yellow,
That there fell out a great dispute
  Between Argyle and Airly.

The Duke o' Montrose has written to Argyle
  To come in the morning early,
An' lead in his men, by the back o' Dunkeld,
  To plunder the bonnie house o' Airly.

The lady look'd o'er her window sae hie,
  And O but she looked weary!
And there she espied the great Argyle
  Come to plunder the bonnie house o' Airly.

"Come down, come down, Lady Margaret," he says,
  "Come down and kiss me fairly,
Or before the morning clear daylight,
  I'll no leave a standing stane in Airly."

"I wadna kiss thee, great Argyle,
  I wadna kiss thee fairly,
I wadna kiss thee, great Argyle,
  Gin you shouldna leave a standing stane in Airly."

He has ta'en her by the middle sae sma',
  Says "Lady, where is your drury?"
"It's up and down by the bonnie burn side,
  Amang the planting of Airly."

They sought it up, they sought it down,
    They sought it late and early,
And found it in the bonnie balm-tree,
    That shines on the bowling-green o' Airly.

He has ta'en her by the left shoulder,
    And O but she grat sairly,
And led her down to yon green bank,
    Till he plundered the bonnie house o' Airly.

"O it's I hae seven braw sons," she says,
    "And the youngest ne'er saw his daddie,
And altho' I had as mony mae,
    I wad gie them a' to Charlie.

"But gin my good lord had been at hame,
    As this night he is wi' Charlie,
There durst na a Campbell in a' the west
    Hae plundered the bonnie house o' Airly."

ROB ROY

(Child, vol. vi. Early Edition.)

Rob Roy from the Highlands cam,
    Unto the Lawlan' border,
To steal awa a gay ladie
    To haud his house in order.
He cam oure the lock o' Lynn,
    Twenty men his arms did carry;
Himsel gaed in, an' fand her out,
    Protesting he would marry.

"O will ye gae wi' me," he says,
    "Or will ye be my honey?
Or will ye be my wedded wife?
    For I love you best of any."
"I winna gae wi' you," she says,
    "Nor will I be your honey,
Nor will I be your wedded wife;
    You love me for my money."

. . . . .

But he set her on a coal-black steed,
    Himsel lap on behind her,
An' he's awa to the Highland hills,
    Whare her frien's they canna find her.

. . . . .

"Rob Roy was my father ca'd,
    Macgregor was his name, ladie;
He led a band o' heroes bauld,
    An' I am here the same, ladie.
Be content, be content,
    Be content to stay, ladie,
For thou art my wedded wife
    Until thy dying day, ladie.

"He was a hedge unto his frien's,
  A heckle to his foes, ladie,
Every one that durst him wrang,
  He took him by the nose, ladie.
I'm as bold, I'm as bold,
  I'm as bold, an more, ladie;
He that daurs dispute my word,
  Shall feel my guid claymore, ladie."

THE BATTLE OF KILLIE-CRANKIE

(*Child*, vol. vii. Early Edition.)

CLAVERS and his Highlandmen
  Came down upo' the raw, man,
Who being stout, gave mony a clout;
  The lads began to claw then.
With sword and terge into their hand,
  Wi which they were nae slaw, man,
Wi mony a fearful heavy sigh,
  The lads began to claw then.

O'er bush, o'er bank, o'er ditch, o'er stark,
  She flang amang them a', man;
The butter-box got many knocks,
  Their riggings paid for a' then.
They got their paiks, wi sudden straiks,
  Which to their grief they saw, man:
Wi clinkum, clankum o'er their crowns,
  The lads began to fa' then.

Hur skipt about, hur leapt about,
  And flang amang them a', man;
The English blades got broken heads,
  'Their crowns were cleav'd in twa then.
The durk and door made their last hour,
  And prov'd their final fa', man;
They thought the devil had been there,
  That play'd them sic a paw then.

The Solemn League and Covenant
   Came whigging up the hills, man;
Thought Highland trews durst not refuse
   For to subscribe their bills then.
In Willie's name, they thought nae ane
   Durst stop their course at a', man,
But hur-nane-sell, wi mony a knock,
   Cry'd "Furich—Whigs awa'," man.

Sir Evan Du, and his men true,
   Came linking up the brink, man;
The Hogan Dutch they feared such,
   They bred a horrid stink then.
The true Maclean and his fierce men
   Came in amang them a', man;
Nane durst withstand his heavy hand,
   All fled and ran awa' then.

Oh' on a ri, Oh' on a ri,
   Why should she lose King Shames, man?
Oh' rig in di, Oh' rig in di,
   She shall break a' her banes then;
With *furichinish*, an' stay a while,
   And speak a word or twa, man,
She's gi' a straike, out o'er the neck,
   Before ye win awa' then.

Oh fy for shame, ye're three for ane,
   Hur-nane-sell's won the day, man;
King Shames' red-coats should be hung up,
   Because they ran awa' then.
Had bent their brows, like Highland trows,
   And made as lang a stay, man,
They'd sav'd their king, that sacred thing,
   And Willie 'd ran awa' then.

ANNAN WATER.

(*Child,* vol. ii.   Early Edition.)

"ANNAN water's wading deep,
   And my love Annie's wondrous bonny;
And I am laith she suld weet her feet,
   Because I love her best of ony.

"Gar saddle me the bonny black,—
   Gar saddle sune, and make him ready:
For I will down the Gatehope-Slack,
   And all to see my bonny ladye."—

He has loupen on the bonny black,
   He stirr'd him wi' the spur right sairly;
But, or he wan the Gatehope-Slack,
   I think the steed was wae and weary.

He has loupen on the bonny gray,
   He rade the right gate and the ready;
I trow he would neither stint nor stay,
   For he was seeking his bonny ladye.

O he has ridden o'er field and fell,
   Through muir and moss, and mony a mire;
His spurs o' steel were sair to bide,
   And fra her fore-feet flew the fire.

"Now, bonny grey, now play your part!
   Gin ye be the steed that wins my deary,
Wi' corn and hay ye'se be fed for aye,
   And never spur sall make you wearie."

The gray was a mare, and a right good mare;
    But when she wan the Annan water,
She couldna hae ridden a furlong mair,
    Had a thousand merks been wadded at her.

"O boatman, boatman, put off your boat!
    Put off your boat for gowden monie!
I cross the drumly stream the night,
    Or never mair I see my honey."—

"O I was sworn sae late yestreen,
    And not by ae aith, but by many;
And for a' the gowd in fair Scotland,
    I dare na take ye through to Annie."

The side was stey, and the bottom deep,
    Frae bank to brae the water pouring;
And the bonny grey mare did sweat for fear,
    For she heard the water-kelpy roaring.

O he has pou'd aff his dapperpy coat,
    The silver buttons glancèd bonny;
The waistcoat bursted aff his breast,
    He was sae full of melancholy.

He has ta'en the ford at that stream tail;
    I wot he swam both strong and steady;
But the stream was broad, and his strength did fail,
    And he never saw his bonny ladye.

"O wae betide the frush saugh wand!
    And wae betide the bush of brier!
It brake into my true love's hand,
    When his strength did fail, and his limbs did tire.

"And wae betide ye, Annan water,
    This night that ye are a drumlie river!
For over thee I'll build a bridge,
    That ye never more true love may sever."—

THE ELPHIN NOURRICE
(C. K. Sharpe.)

I HEARD a cow low, a bonnie cow low,
  An' a cow low down in yon glen;
Lang, lang will my young son greet,
  Or his mither bid him come ben.

I heard a cow low, a bonnie cow low,
  An' a cow low down in yon fauld;
Lang, lang will my young son greet,
  Or his mither take him frae cauld.

  Waken, Queen of Elfan,
  An hear your Nourrice moan.
  O moan ye for your meat,
  Or moan ye for your fee,
  Or moan ye for the ither bounties
  That ladies are wont to gie?

I moan na for my meat,
  Nor yet for my fee,
But I mourn for Christened land—
  It's there I fain would be.

O nurse my bairn, Nourice, she says,
  Till he stan' at your knee,
An' ye's win hame to Christen land,
  Whar fain it's ye wad be.

O keep my bairn, Nourice,
  Till he gang by the hauld,
An' ye's win hame to your young son,
  Ye left in four nights auld.

COSPATRICK

(*Mackay.*)

Cospatrick has sent o'er the faem ;
Cospatrick brought his ladye hame ;
And fourscore ships have come her wi',
The ladye by the green-wood tree.

There were twal' and twal' wi' baken bread,
And twal' and twal' wi' gowd sae red,
And twal' and twal' wi' bouted flour,
And twal' and twal' wi' the paramour.

Sweet Willy was a widow's son,
And at her stirrup he did run ;
And she was clad in the finest pall,
But aye she loot the tears down fall.

" O is your saddle set awrye ?
Or rides your steed for you owre high ?
Or are you mourning, in your tide,
That you suld be Cospatrick's bride ? "

" I am not mourning, at this tide,
That I suld be Cospatrick's bride ;
But I am sorrowing in my mood,
That I suld leave my mother good."

" But, gentle boy, come tell to me,
What is the custom of thy countrie ? "
" The custom thereof, my dame," he says,
" Will ill a gentle ladye please.

"Seven king's daughters has our lord wedded,
And seven king's daughters has our lord bedded;
But he's cutted their breasts frae their breast-bane,
And sent them mourning hame again.

Yet, gin you're sure that you're a maid,
Ye may gae safely to his bed;
But gif o' that ye be na sure,
Then hire some damsel o' your bour."

The ladye's called her bour-maiden,
That waiting was unto her train.
"Five thousand marks I'll gie to thee,
To sleep this night with my lord for me."

When bells were rung, and mass was sayne,
And a' men unto bed were gane,
Cospatrick and the bonny maid,
Into ae chamber they were laid.

"Now speak to me, blankets, and speak to me, bed,
And speak, thou sheet, enchanted web;
And speak, my sword, that winna lie,
Is this a true maiden that lies by me?"

"It is not a maid that you hae wedded,
But it is a maid that you hae bedded;
It is a leal maiden that lies by thee,
But not the maiden that it should be."

O wrathfully he left the bed,
And wrathfully his claes on did;
And he has ta'en him through the ha',
And on his mother he did ca'.

"I am the most unhappy man,
That ever was in Christen land?
I courted a maiden, meik and mild,
And I hae gotten naething but a woman wi' child."

"O stay, my son, into this ha',
And sport ye wi' your merry men a';
And I will to the secret bour,
To see how it fares wi' your paramour."

The carline she was stark and stare,
She aff the hinges dang the dure.
"O is your bairn to laird or loun,
Or is it to your father's groom?"

"O hear me, mother, on my knee,
Till my sad story I tell to thee:
O we were sisters, sisters seven,
We were the fairest under heaven.

"It fell on a summer's afternoon,
When a' our toilsome work was done,
We coost the kevils us amang,
To see which suld to the green-wood gang.

"Ohon! alas, for I was youngest,
And aye my weird it was the strongest!
The kevil it on me did fa',
Whilk was the cause of a' my woe.

"For to the green-wood I maun gae,
To pu' the red rose and the slae;
To pu' the red rose and the thyme,
To deck my mother's bour and mine.

"I hadna pu'd a flower but ane,
When by there came a gallant hinde,
Wi' high colled hose and laigh colled shoon,
And he seemed to be some king's son.

"And be I maid, or be I nae,
He kept me there till the close o' day;
And be I maid, or be I nane,
He kept me there till the day was done.

"He gae me a lock o' his yellow hair,
And bade me keep it ever mair;
He gae me a carknet o' bonny beads,
And bade me keep it against my needs.

"He gae to me a gay gold ring,
And bade me keep it abune a' thing."
"What did ye wi' the tokens rare,
That ye gat frae that gallant there?"

"O bring that coffer unto me,
And a' the tokens ye sall see."
"Now stay, daughter, your bour within,
While I gae parley wi' my son."

O she has ta'en her thro' the ha',
And on her son began to ca':
"What did ye wi' the bonny beads,
I bade ye keep against your needs?

"What did you wi' the gay gold ring,
I bade you keep abune a' thing?"
"I gae them to a ladye gay,
I met in green-wood on a day.

"But I wad gie a' my halls and tours,
I had that ladye within my bours,
But I wad gie my very life,
I had that ladye to my wife."

"Now keep, my son, your ha's and tours;
Ye have that bright burd in your bours;
And keep, my son, your very life;
Ye have that ladye to your wife."

Now, or a month was come and gane,
The ladye bore a bonny son;
And 'twas written on his breast bane,
"Cospatrick is my father's name."

JOHNNIE ARMSTRANG

Some speak of lords, some speak of lairds,
    And sic like men of high degree;
Of a gentleman I sing a sang,
    Some time call'd Laird of Gilnockie.

The king he writes a loving letter,
    With his ain hand sae tenderlie,
And he hath sent it to Johnnie Armstrang,
    To come and speak with him speedilie.

The Elliots and Armstrangs did convene,
    They were a gallant companie:
"We'll ride and meet our lawful king,
    And bring him safe to Gilnockie.

"Make kinnen [1] and capon ready, then,
    And venison in great plentie;
We'll welcome here our royal king;
    I hope he'll dine at Gilnockie!"

They ran their horse on the Langholm howm,
    And brake their spears with meikle main;
The ladies lookit frae their loft windows—
    "God bring our men weel hame again!"

When Johnnie came before the king,
    With all his men sae brave to see,
The king he moved his bonnet to him;
    He ween'd he was a king as well as he.

[1] "Kinnen," rabbits.

"May I find grace, my sovereign liege,
  Grace for my loyal men and me?
For my name it is Johnnie Armstrang,
  And a subject of yours, my liege," said he.

"Away, away, thou traitor strang!
  Out of my sight soon may'st thou be!
I granted never a traitor's life,
  And now I'll not begin with thee."

"Grant me my life, my liege, my king!
  And a bonnie gift I'll gi'e to thee;
Full four-and-twenty milk-white steeds,
  Were all foal'd in ae year to me.

"I ll gi'e thee all these milk-white steeds,
  That prance and nicher [1] at a spear;
And as meikle gude Inglish gilt,[2]
  As four of their braid backs dow [3] bear."

"Away, away, thou traitor strang!
  Out of my sight soon may'st thou be!
I granted never a traitor's life,
  And now I'll not begin with thee."

"Grant me my life, my liege, my king!
  And a bonnie gift I'll gi'e to thee:
Gude four-and-twenty ganging [4] mills,
  That gang thro' all the year to me.

"These four-and-twenty mills complete,
  Shall gang for thee thro' all the year;
And as meikle of gude red wheat,
  As all their happers dow to bear."

[1] "Nicher," neigh.   [2] "Gilt," gold.
[3] "Dow," are able to.   [4] "Ganging," going.

"Away, away, thou traitor strang!
  Out of my sight soon may'st thou be!
I granted never a traitor's life,
  And now I'll not begin with thee."

"Grant me my life, my liege, my king!
  And a great gift I'll gi'e to thee:
Bauld four-and-twenty sisters' sons
  Shall for thee fecht, tho' all shou'd flee."

"Away, away, thou traitor strang!
  Out of my sight soon may'st thou be!
I granted never a traitor's life,
  And now I'll not begin with thee."

"Grant me my life, my liege, my king!
  And a brave gift I'll gi'e to thee:
All between here and Newcastle town
  Shall pay their yearly rent to thee."

"Away, away, thou traitor strang!
  Out of my sight soon may'st thou be!
I granted never a traitor's life,
  And now I'll not begin with thee."

"Ye lied, ye lied, now, king," he says,
  "Altho' a king and prince ye be!
For I've loved naething in my life,
  I weel dare say it, but honestie.

"Save a fat horse, and a fair woman,
  Twa bonnie dogs to kill a deer;
But England shou'd have found me meal and mault,
  Gif I had lived this hundred year.

"She shou'd have found me meal and mault,
  And beef and mutton in all plentie;
But never a Scots wife cou'd have said,
  That e'er I skaith'd her a puir flee.

"To seek het water beneath cauld ice,
　　Surely it is a great follie:
I have ask'd grace at a graceless face,
　　But there is nane for my men and me.

"But had I kenn'd, ere I came frae hame,
　　How unkind thou wou'dst been to me,
I wou'd ha'e keepit the Border side,
　　In spite of all thy force and thee.

"Wist England's king that I was ta'en,
　　Oh, gin a blythe man he wou'd be!
For ance I slew his sister's son,
　　And on his breast-bane brak a tree."

John wore a girdle about his middle,
　　Embroider'd o'er with burning gold,
Bespangled with the same metal,
　　Maist beautiful was to behold.

There hang nine targats [1] at Johnnie's hat,
　　An ilk ane worth three hundred pound:
"What wants that knave that a king shou'd have,
　　But the sword of honour and the crown?

"Oh, where got thee these targats, Johnnie,
　　That blink sae brawly [2] aboon thy brie?"
"I gat them in the field fechting,[3]
　　Where, cruel king, thou durst not be.

"Had I my horse and harness gude,
　　And riding as I wont to be,
It shou'd have been tauld this hundred year,
　　The meeting of my king and me!

　　　[1] "Targats," tassels.
　　　[2] "Blink sae brawly," glance so bravely.
　　　[3] "Fechting," fighting.

"God be with thee, Kirsty,[1] my brother,
  Lang live thou laird of Mangertoun !
Lang may'st thou live on the Border side,
  Ere thou see thy brother ride up and down !

"And God be with thee, Kirsty, my son,
  Where thou sits on thy nurse's knee !
But an thou live this hundred year,
  Thy father's better thou'lt never be.

"Farewell, my bonnie Gilnock hall,
  Where on Esk side thou standest stout !
Gif I had lived but seven years mair,
  I wou'd ha'e gilt thee round about."

John murder'd was at Carlinrigg,
  And all his gallant companie ;
But Scotland's heart was ne'er sae wae,
  To see sae mony brave men die ;

Because they saved their country dear
  Frae Englishmen ! Nane were sae bauld ;
While Johnnie lived on the Border side,
  Nane of them durst come near his hauld.

[1] "Kirsty," Christopher.

EDOM O' GORDON

It fell about the Martinmas,
    When the wind blew shrill and cauld,
Said Edom o' Gordon to his men,—
    "We maun draw to a hald.[1]

"And whatna hald shall we draw to,
    My merry men and me?
We will gae straight to Towie house,
    To see that fair ladye."

[The ladye stood on her castle wall,
    Beheld baith dale and down;
There she was 'ware of a host of men
    Came riding towards the town.

"Oh, see ye not, my merry men all,
    Oh, see ye not what I see?
Methinks I see a host of men;
    I marvel who they be."

She thought it had been her own wed lord,
    As he came riding hame;
It was the traitor, Edom o' Gordon,
    Wha reck'd nae sin nor shame.]

She had nae sooner buskit hersel',
    And putten on her gown,
Till Edom o' Gordon and his men
    Were round about the town.

[1] "Hald," hold.

They had nae sooner supper set,
  Nae sooner said the grace,
Till Edom o' Gordon and his men
  Were round about the place.

The ladye ran to her tower head,
  As fast as she cou'd hie,
To see if, by her fair speeches,
  She cou'd with him agree.

As soon as he saw this ladye fair,
  And her yetts all lockit fast,
He fell into a rage of wrath,
  And his heart was all aghast.

"Come down to me, ye ladye gay,
  Come down, come down to me;
This night ye shall lye within my arms,
  The morn my bride shall be."

"I winna come down, ye false Gordon,
  I winna come down to thee;
I winna forsake my ain dear lord,
  That is sae far frae me."

"Gi'e up your house, ye ladye fair,
  Gi'e up your house to me;
Or I shall burn yoursel' therein,
  Bot and your babies three."

"I winna gi'e up, ye false Gordon,
  To nae sic traitor as thee;
Tho' you shou'd burn mysel' therein,
  Bot and my babies three.

["But fetch to me my pistolette,
  And charge to me my gun;
For, but if I pierce that bluidy butcher,
  My babes we will be undone."

She stiffly stood on her castle wall,
    And let the bullets flee;
She miss'd that bluidy butcher's heart,
    Tho' she slew other three.]

"Set fire to the house!" quo' the false
    Gordon,
    "Since better may nae be;
And I will burn hersel' therein,
    Bot and her babies three."

"Wae worth, wae worth ye, Jock, my
    man,
    I paid ye weel your fee;
Why pull ye out the grund-wa'-stane,
    Lets in the reek [1] to me?

"And e'en wae worth ye, Jock, my man,
    I paid ye weel your hire;
Why pull ye out my grund-wa'-stane,
    To me lets in the fire?"

"Ye paid me weel my hire, ladye,
    Ye paid me weel my fee;
But now I'm Edom o' Gordon's man,
    Maun either do or dee."

Oh, then out spake her youngest son,
    Sat on the nurse's knee:
Says—"Mither dear, gi'e o'er this house,
    For the reek it smothers me."

["I wou'd gi'e all my gold, my bairn,
    Sae wou'd I all my fee,
For ae blast of the westlin' wind,
    To blaw the reek frae thee.]

[1] "Reek," smoke.

"But I winna gi'e up my house, my dear,
   To nae sic traitor as he;
Come weal, come woe, my jewels fair,
   Ye maun take share with me."

Oh, then out spake her daughter dear,
   She was baith jimp and small:
"Oh, row me in a pair of sheets,
   And tow me o'er the wall."

They row'd her in a pair of sheets,
   And tow'd her o'er the wall;
But on the point of Gordon's spear
   She got a deadly fall.

Oh, bonnie, bonnie was her mouth,
   And cherry were her cheeks;
And clear, clear was her yellow hair,
   Whereon the red bluid dreeps.

Then with his spear he turn'd her o'er,
   Oh, gin her face was wan!
He said—"You are the first that e'er
   I wish'd alive again."

He turn'd her o'er and o'er again,
   Oh, gin her skin was white!
"I might ha'e spared that bonnie face
   To ha'e been some man's delight.

"Busk and boun, my merry men all,
   For ill dooms I do guess;
I canna look on that bonnie face,
   As it lyes on the grass!"

"Wha looks to freits,[1] my master dear,
   Their freits will follow them;
Let it ne'er be said brave Edom o' Gordon
   Was daunted with a dame."

[1] "Freits," omens.

[But when the ladye saw the fire
    Come flaming o'er her head,
She wept, and kissed her children twain ;
    Said—"Bairns, we been but dead."

The Gordon then his bugle blew,
    And said—"Away, away !
The house of Towie is all in a flame,
    I hald it time to gae."]

Oh, then he spied her ain dear lord,
    As he came o'er the lea ;
He saw his castle all in a flame,
    As far as he could see.

Then sair, oh sair his mind misgave,
    And oh, his heart was wae !
"Put on, put on, my wighty [1] men,
    As fast as ye can gae.

"Put on, put on, my wighty men,
    As fast as ye can drie ;
For he that is hindmost of the thrang
    Shall ne'er get gude of me !"

Then some they rade, and some they ran,
    Full fast out o'er the bent ;
But ere the foremost could win up,
    Baith ladye and babes were brent.

[He wrang his hands, he rent his hair,
    And wept in tearful mood ;
"Ah, traitors ! for this cruel deed,
    Ye shall weep tears of bluid."

And after the Gordon he has gane,
    Sae fast as he might drie ;
And soon in the Gordon's foul heart's bluid
    He's wroken [2] his dear layde.]

[1] "Wighty," valiant.   [2] "Wroken," revenged.

And mony were the mudie[1] men,
　　Lay gasping on the green;
And mony were the fair ladyes
　　Lay lemanless at hame.

And mony were the mudie men
　　Lay gasping on the green;
For of fifty men the Gordon brocht,
　　There were but five gaed hame.

And round, and round the walls he went,
　　Their ashes for to view;
At last into the flames he flew,
　　And bade the world adieu.

[1] "Mudie," bold.

LADY ANNE BOTHWELL'S LAMENT

(*Child*, vol. iv. Early Edition.)

BALOW, my boy, ly still and sleep,
It grieves me sore to hear thee weep,
If thou'lt be silent, I'll be glad,
Thy mourning makes my heart full sad.
Balow, my boy, thy mother's joy,
Thy father bred one great annoy.
    Balow, my boy, ly still and sleep,
    It grieves me sore to hear thee weep.

Balow, my darling, sleep a while,
And when thou wak'st then sweetly smile;
But smile not as thy father did,
To cozen maids, nay, God forbid;
For in thine eye his look I see,
The tempting look that ruin'd me.
    Balow, my boy, etc.

When he began to court my love,
And with his sugar'd words to move,
His tempting face, and flatt'ring chear,
In time to me did not appear;
But now I see that cruel he
Cares neither for his babe nor me.
    Balow, my boy, etc.

Fareweel, fareweel, thou falsest youth
That ever kist a woman's mouth.
Let never any after me
Submit unto thy courtesy!
For, if they do, O! cruel thou
Wilt her abuse and care not how!
    Balow, my boy, etc.

I was too cred'lous at the first,
To yield thee all a maiden durst.
Thou swore for ever true to prove,
Thy faith unchang'd, unchang'd thy love;
But quick as thought the change is wrought,
Thy love's no mair, thy promise nought.
    Balow, my boy, etc.

I wish I were a maid again!
From young men's flatt'ry I'd refrain;
For now unto my grief I find
They all are perjur'd and unkind;
Bewitching charms bred all my harms;—
Witness my babe lies in my arms.
    Balow, my boy, etc.

I take my fate from bad to worse,
That I must needs be now a nurse,
And lull my young son on my lap:
From me, sweet orphan, take the pap.
Balow, my child, thy mother mild
Shall wail as from all bliss exil'd.
    Balow, my boy, etc.

Balow, my boy, weep not for me,
Whose greatest grief's for wronging thee.
Nor pity her deserved smart,
Who can blame none but her fond heart;
For, too soon trusting latest finds
With fairest tongues are falsest minds.
    Balow, my boy, etc.

Balow, my boy, thy father's fled,
When he the thriftless son has played;
Of vows and oaths forgetful, he
Preferr'd the wars to thee and me.
But now, perhaps, thy curse and mine
Make him eat acorns with the swine.
   Balow, my boy, etc.

But curse not him; perhaps now he,
Stung with remorse, is blessing thee:
Perhaps at death; for who can tell
Whether the judge of heaven or hell,
By some proud foe has struck the blow,
And laid the dear deceiver low?
   Balow, my boy, etc.

I wish I were into the bounds
Where he lies smother'd in his wounds,
Repeating, as he pants for air,
My name, whom once he call'd his fair;
No woman's yet so fiercely set
But she'll forgive, though not forget.
   Balow, my boy, etc.

If linen lacks, for my love's sake
Then quickly to him would I make
My smock, once for his body meet,
And wrap him in that winding-sheet.
Ah me! how happy had I been,
If he had ne'er been wrapt therein.
   Balow, my boy, etc.

Balow, my boy, I'll weep for thee;
Too soon, alake, thou'lt weep for me:
Thy griefs are growing to a sum,
God grant thee patience when they come;
Born to sustain thy mother's shame,
A hapless fate, a bastard's name.
   Balow, my boy, ly still and sleep,
   It grieves me sore to hear thee weep.

JOCK O THE SIDE

(*Child*, Part VI., p. 479.)

Now Liddisdale has ridden a raid,
  But I wat they had better staid at hame ;
For Mitchell o Winfield he is dead,
  And my son Johnie is prisner tane?
    With my fa ding diddle, la la dow diddle.

For Mangerton house auld Downie is gane,
  Her coats she has kilted up to her knee ;
And down the water wi speed she rins,
  While tears in spaits fa fast frae her eie.

Then up and bespake the lord Mangerton :
  "What news, what news, sister Downie, to me ?"
"Bad news, bad news, my lord Mangerton ;
  Mitchel is killd, and tane they hae my son Johnie."

"Neer fear, sister Downie," quo Mangerton ;
  "I hae yokes of oxen, four-and-twentie,
My barns, my byres, and my faulds, a' weel filld,
  And I'll part wi them a' ere Johnie shall die.

"Three men I'll take to set him free,
  Weel harnessd a' wi best of steel ;
The English rogues may hear, and drie
  The weight o their braid swords to feel.

"The Laird's Jock ane, the Laird's Wat twa,
  O Hobie Noble, thou ane maun be!
Thy coat is blue, thou has been true,
  Since England banishd thee, to me."

Now, Hobie was an English man,
  In Bewcastle-dale was bred and born;
But his misdeeds they were sae great,
  They banished him neer to return.

Lord Mangerton then orders gave,—
  "Your horses the wrang way maun a' be shod;
Like gentlemen ye must not seem,
  But look like corn-caugers gawn ae road.

"Your armour gude ye maunna shaw,
  Nor ance appear like men o weir;
As country lads be all arrayd,
  Wi branks and brecham on ilk mare."

Sae now a' their horses are shod the wrang way,
  And Hobie has mounted his grey sae fine,
Jock his lively bay, Wat's on his white horse behind,
  And on they rode for the water o Tyne.

At the Cholerford they a' light down,
  And there, wi the help o the light o the moon,
A tree they cut, wi fifteen naggs upon each side,
  To climb up the wall of Newcastle toun.

But when they came to Newcastle toun,
  And were alighted at the wa,
They fand their tree three ells oer laigh,
  They fand their stick baith short and sma.

Then up and spake the Laird's ain Jock,
  "There's naething for't; the gates we maun force."
But when they cam the gate unto,
  A proud porter withstood baith men and horse.

His neck in twa I wat they hae wrung;
  Wi foot or hand he neer play'd paw;
His life and his keys at anes they hae taen,
  And cast his body ahind the wa.

Now soon they reached Newcastle jail,
  And to the prisner thus they call:
"Sleips thou, wakes thou, Jock o the Side,
  Or is thou wearied o thy thrall?"

Jock answers thus, wi dolefu tone:
  "Aft, aft I wake, I seldom sleip;
But wha's this kens my name sae weel,
  And thus to hear my waes does seek?"

Then up and spake the good Laird's Jock:
  "Neer fear ye now, my billie," quo he;
"For here's the Laird's Jock, the Laird's Wat,
  And Hobie Noble, come to set thee free."

"Oh, had thy tongue, and speak nae mair,
  And o thy talk now let me be!
For if a' Liddesdale were here the night,
  The morn's the day that I maun die.

"Full fifteen stane o Spanish iron,
  They hae laid a' right sair on me;
Wi locks and keys I am fast bound
  Into this dungeon mirk and drearie."

"Fear ye no that," quo the Laird's Jock;
  "A faint heart neer wan a fair ladie;
Work thou within, we'll work without,
  And I'll be sworn we set thee free."

The first strong dore that they came at,
  They loosed it without a key;
The next chaind dore that they cam at,
  They gard it a' in flinders flee.

The prisner now, upo his back,
  The Laird's Jock's gotten up fu hie;
And down the stair him, irons and a',
  Wi nae sma speed and joy brings he.

"Now, Jock, I wat," quo Hobie Noble,
  "Part o the weight ye may lay on me;"
"I wat weel no," quo the Laird's Jock,
  "I count him lighter than a flee."

Sae out at the gates they a' are gane,
  The prisner's set on horseback hie;
And now wi speed they've tane the gate;
  While ilk ane jokes fu wantonlie.

"O Jock, sae winsomely's ye ride,
  Wi baith your feet upo ae side!
Sae weel's ye're harnessd, and sae trig!
  In troth ye sit like ony bride."

The night, tho wat, they didna mind,
  But hied them on fu mirrilie,
Until they cam to Cholerford brae,
  Where the water ran like mountains hie.

But when they came to Cholerford,
  There they met with an auld man;
Says, "Honest man, will the water ride?
  Tell us in haste, if that ye can."

"I wat weel no," quo the good auld man;
"Here I hae livd this threty yeirs and three,
And I neer yet saw the Tyne sae big,
Nor rinning ance sae like a sea."

Then up and spake the Laird's saft Wat,
The greatest coward in the company;
"Now halt, now halt, we needna try't;
The day is comd we a' maun die!"

"Poor faint-hearted thief!" quo the Laird's Jock,
"There'll nae man die but he that's fie;
I'll lead ye a' right safely through;
Lift ye the prisner on ahint me."

Sae now the water they a' hae tane,
By anes and twas they a' swam through;
"Here are we a' safe," says the Laird's Jock,
"And, poor faint Wat, what think ye now?"

They scarce the ither side had won,
When twenty men they saw pursue;
Frae Newcastle town they had been sent,
A' English lads right good and true.

But when the land-sergeant the water saw,
"It winna ride, my lads," quo he;
Then out he cries, "Ye the prisner may take,
But leave the irons, I pray, to me."

"I wat weel no," cryd the Laird's Jock,
"I'll keep them a'; shoon to my mare they'll be;
My good grey mare; for I am sure,
She's bought them a' fu dear frae thee."

Sae now they're away for Liddisdale,
    Een as fast as they coud them hie ;
The prisner's brought to his ain fireside,
    And there o's airns they make him free.

" Now, Jock, my billie," quo a' the three,
    " The day was comd thou was to die ;
But thou 's as weel at thy ain fireside,
    Now sitting, I think, 'tween thee and me."

They hae gard fill up ae punch-bowl,
    And after it they maun hae anither,
And thus the night they a' hae spent,
    Just as they had been brither and brither.

LORD THOMAS AND FAIR ANNET

(*Child*, Part III., p. 182.)

LORD THOMAS and Fair Annet
   Sate a' day on a hill;
Whan night was cum, and sun was sett,
   They had not talkt their fill.

Lord Thomas said a word in jest,
   Fair Annet took it ill:
"A, I will nevir wed a wife
   Against my ain friend's will."

"Gif ye wull nevir wed a wife,
   A wife wull neir wed yee;"
Sae he is hame to tell his mither,
   And knelt upon his knee.

"O rede, O rede, mither," he says,
   "A gude rede gie to mee;
O sall I tak the nut-browne bride,
   And let Faire Annet bee?"

"The nut-browne bride haes gowd and gear,
   Fair Annet she has gat nane;
And the little beauty Fair Annet haes
   O it wull soon be gane."

And he has till his brother gane:
   "Now, brother, rede ye mee;
A, sall I marrie the nut-browne bride,
   And let Fair Annet bee?"

"The nut-browne bride has oxen, brother,
   The nut-browne bride has kye;
I wad·hae ye marrie the nut-browne bride,
   And cast Fair Annet bye."

"Her oxen may dye i' the house, billie,
   And her kye into the byre;
And I sall hae nothing to mysell
   Bot a fat fadge by the fyre."

And he has till his sister gane:
   "Now, sister, rede ye mee;
O sall I marrie the nut-browne bride,
   And set Fair Annet free?"

"I'se rede ye tak Fair Annet, Thomas,
   And let the browne bride alane;
Lest ye sould sigh, and say, Alace,
   What is this we brought hame!"

"No, I will tak my mither's counsel,
   And marrie me owt o hand;
And I will tak the nut-browne bride,
   Fair Annet may leive the land."

Up then rose Fair Annet's father,
   Twa hours or it wer day,
And he is gane unto the bower
   Wherein Fair Annet lay.

'Rise up, rise up, Fair Annet," he says,
   "Put on your silken sheene;
Let us gae to St. Marie's Kirke,
   And see that rich weddeen."

"My maides, gae to my dressing-roome,
   And dress to me my hair;
Whaireir yee laid a plait before,
   See yee lay ten times mair.

"My maids, gae to my dressing-room,
　And dress to me my smock;
The one half is o the holland fine,
　The other o needle-work."

The horse Fair Annet rade upon,
　He amblit like the wind;
Wi siller he was shod before,
　Wi burning gowd behind.

Four and twanty siller bells
　Wer a' tyed till his mane,
And yae tift o the norland wind,
　They tinkled ane by ane.

Four and twanty gay gude knichts
　Rade by Fair Annet's side,
And four and twanty fair ladies,
　As gin she had bin a bride.

And whan she cam to Marie's Kirk,
　She sat on Marie's stean:
The cleading that Fair Annet had on
　It skinkled in their een.

And whan she cam into the kirk,
　She shimmerd like the sun;
The belt that was about her waist
　Was a' wi pearles bedone.

She sat her by the nut-browne bride,
　And her een they wer sae clear,
Lord Thomas he clean forgat the bride,
　When Fair Annet drew near.

He had a rose into his hand,
　He gae it kisses three,
And reaching by the nut-browne bride,
　Laid it on Fair Annet's knee.

Up then spak the nut-browne bride,
   She spak wi meikle spite:
"And whair gat ye that rose-water,
   That does mak yee sae white?"

"O I did get the rose-water
   Whair ye wull neir get nane,
For I did get that very rose-water
   Into my mither's wame."

The bride she drew a long bodkin
   Frae out her gay head-gear,
And strake Fair Annet unto the heart,
   That word spak nevir mair.

Lord Thomas he saw Fair Annet wex pale,
   And marvelit what mote bee;
But when he saw her dear heart's blude,
   A' wood-wroth wexed hee.

He drew his dagger that was sae sharp,
   That was sae sharp and meet,
And drave it into the nut-browne bride,
   That fell deid at his feit.

"Now stay for me, dear Annet," he sed,
   "Now stay, my dear," he cry'd;
Then strake the dagger untill his heart,
   And fell deid by her side.

Lord Thomas was buried without kirk-wa,
   Fair Annet within the quiere,
And o the ane thair grew a birk,
   The other a bonny briere.

And ay they grew, and ay they threw,
   As they wad faine be neare;
And by this ye may ken right weil
   They were twa luvers deare.

FAIR ANNIE

(*Child*, Part III., p. 69.)

" It's narrow, narrow, make your bed,
 And learn to lie your lane ;
For I'm ga'n oer the sea, Fair Annie,
 A braw bride to bring hame.
Wi her I will get gowd and gear ;
 Wi you I neer got nane.

" But wha will bake my bridal bread,
 Or brew my bridal ale?
And wha will welcome my brisk bride,
 That I bring oer the dale?"

" It's I will bake your bridal bread,
 And brew your bridal ale,
And I will welcome your brisk bride,
 That you bring oer the dale."

" But she that welcomes my brisk bride
 Maun gang like maiden fair ;
She maun lace on her robe sae jimp,
 And braid her yellow hair."

" But how can I gang maiden-like,
 When maiden I am nane?
Have I not born seven sons to thee,
 And am with child again?"

She's taen her young son in her arms,
    Another in her hand,
And she's up to the highest tower,
    To see him come to land.

"Come up, come up, my eldest son,
    And look oer yon sea-strand,
And see your father's new-come bride,
    Before she come to land."

"Come down, come down, my mother dear,
    Come frae the castle wa !
I fear, if langer ye stand there,
    Ye'll let yoursell down fa."

And she gaed down, and farther down,
    Her love's ship for to see,
And the topmast and the mainmast
    Shone like the silver free.

And she's gane down, and farther down,
    The bride's ship to behold,
And the topmast and the mainmast
    They shone just like the gold.

She's taen her seven sons in her hand,
    I wot she didna fail ;
She met Lord Thomas and his bride,
    As they came oer the dale.

"You're welcome to your house, Lord Thomas,
    You're welcome to your land ;
You're welcome with your fair ladye,
    That you lead by the hand.

"You're welcome to your ha's, ladye,
  You're welcome to your bowers;
Your welcome to your hame, ladye,
  For a' that's here is yours."

"I thank thee, Annie; I thank thee, Annie,
  Sae dearly as I thank thee;
You're the likest to my sister Annie,
  That ever I did see.

"There came a knight out oer the sea,
  And steald my sister away;
The shame scoup in his company,
  And land where'er he gae!"

She hang ae napkin at the door,
  Another in the ha,
And a' to wipe the trickling tears,
  Sae fast as they did fa.

And aye she served the lang tables
  With white bread and with wine,
And aye she drank the wan water,
  To had her colour fine.

And aye she served the lang tables,
  With white bread and with brown;
And aye she turned her round about,
  Sae fast the tears fell down.

And he's taen down the silk napkin,
  Hung on a silver pin,
And aye he wipes the tear trickling
  A'down her cheek and chin.

And aye he turn'd him round about,
  And smiled amang his men;
Says, "Like ye best the old ladye,
  Or her that's new come hame?"

When bells were rung, and mass was sung,
   And a' men bound to bed,
Lord Thomas and his new-come bride
   To their chamber they were gaed.

Annie made her bed a little forbye,
   To hear what they might say;
"And ever alas!" Fair Annie cried,
   "That I should see this day!

"Gin my seven sons were seven young rats,
   Running on the castle wa,
And I were a grey cat mysell,
   I soon would worry them a'.

"Gin my young sons were seven young hares,
   Running oer yon lilly lee,
And I were a grew hound mysell,
   Soon worried they a' should be."

And wae and sad Fair Annie sat,
   And drearie was her sang,
And ever, as she sobbd and grat,
   "Wae to the man that did the wrang!"

"My gown is on," said the new-come bride,
   "My shoes are on my feet,
And I will to Fair Annie's chamber,
   And see what gars her greet.

"What ails ye, what ails ye, Fair Annie,
   That ye make sic a moan?
Has your wine-barrels cast the girds,
   Or is your white bread gone?

"O wha was't was your father, Annie,
　　Or wha was't was your mother?
And had ye ony sister, Annie,
　　Or had ye ony brother?"

"The Earl of Wemyss was my father,
　　The Countess of Wemyss my mother;
And a' the folk about the house
　　To me were sister and brother."

"If the Earl of Wemyss was your father,
　　I wot sae was he mine;
And it shall not be for lack o gowd
　　That ye your love sall fyne.

"For I have seven ships o mine ain,
　　A' loaded to the brim,
And I will gie them a' to thee
　　Wi four to thine eldest son:
But thanks to a' the powers in heaven
　　That I gae maiden hame!"

THE DOWIE DENS OF YARROW

(*Child*, Part III.   Early Edition.)

LATE at e'en, drinking the wine,
   And ere they paid the lawing,
They set a combat them between,
   To fight it in the dawing.

"Oh, stay at hame, my noble lord,
   Oh, stay at hame, my marrow!
My cruel brother will you betray
   On the dowie houms of Yarrow."

"Oh, fare ye weel, my ladye gaye!
   Oh, fare ye weel, my Sarah!
For I maun gae, though I ne'er return,
   Frae the dowie banks of Yarrow."

She kiss'd his cheek, she kaim'd his hair,
   As oft she had done before, O;
She belted him with his noble brand,
   And he's away to Yarrow.

As he gaed up the Tennies bank,
   I wot he gaed wi' sorrow,
Till, down in a den, he spied nine arm'd men,
   On the dowie houms of Yarrow.

"Oh, come ye here to part your land,
   The bonnie Forest thorough?
Or come ye here to wield your brand,
   On the dowie houms of Yarrow?"

"I come not here to part my land,
   And neither to beg nor borrow;
I come to wield my noble brand,
   On the bonnie banks of Yarrow.

"If I see all, ye're nine to ane;
   An that's an unequal marrow:
Yet will I fight, while lasts my brand,
   On the bonnie banks of Yarrow."

Four has he hurt, and five has slain,
   On the bloody braes of Yarrow;
'Till that stubborn knight came him behind,
   And ran his body thorough.

"Gae hame, gae hame, good-brother John,
   And tell your sister Sarah,
To come and lift her leafu' lord;
   He's sleepin' sound on Yarrow."

"Yestreen I dream'd a dolefu' dream;
   I fear there will be sorrow!
I dream'd I pu'd the heather green,
   Wi' my true love, on Yarrow.

"O gentle wind, that bloweth south,
   From where my love repaireth,
Convey a kiss from his dear mouth,
   And tell me how he fareth!

"But in the glen strive armed men;
   They've wrought me dole and sorrow;
They've slain—the comeliest knight they've slain—
   He bleeding lies on Yarrow."

As she sped down yon high, high hill,
   She gaed wi' dole and sorrow,
And in the den spied ten slain men,
   On the dowie banks of Yarrow.

She kiss'd his cheek, she kaim'd his hair,
   She search'd his wounds all thorough,
She kiss'd them, till her lips grew red,
   On the dowie houms of Yarrow.

"Now, haud your tongue, my daughter dear!
For a' this breeds but sorrow;
   I'll wed ye to a better lord
Than him ye lost on Yarrow."

"Oh, haud your tongue, my father dear!
   Ye mind me but of sorrow:
A fairer rose did never bloom
   Than now lies cropp'd on Yarrow."

SIR ROLAND

(*Child*, vol. i. Early Edition.)

WHAN he cam to his ain luve's bouir
    He tirled at the pin,
And sae ready was his fair fause luve
    To rise and let him in.

"O welcome, welcome, Sir Roland," she says,
    "Thrice welcome thou art to me;
For this night thou wilt feast in my secret bouir,
    And to-morrow we'll wedded be."

"This night is hallow-eve," he said,
    "And to-morrow is hallow-day;
And I dreamed a drearie dream yestreen,
    That has made my heart fu' wae.

"I dreamed a drearie dream yestreen,
    And I wish it may cum to gude:
I dreamed that ye slew my best grew hound,
    And gied me his lappered blude."

   .   .   .   .

"Unbuckle your belt, Sir Roland," she said,
    "And set you safely down."
"O your chamber is very dark, fair maid,
    And the night is wondrous lown."

"Yes, dark, dark is my secret bouir,
  And lown the midnight may be;
For there is none waking in a' this tower
  But thou, my true love, and me."

. . . .

She has mounted on her true love's steed,
  By the ae light o' the moon;
She has whipped him and spurred him,
  And roundly she rade frae the toun.

She hadna ridden a mile o' gate,
  Never a mile but ane,
When she was aware of a tall young man,
  Slow riding o'er the plain.

She turned her to the right about,
  Then to the left turn'd she;
But aye, 'tween her and the wan moonlight,
  That tall knight did she see.

And he was riding burd alane,
  On a horse as black as jet,
But tho' she followed him fast and fell,
  No nearer could she get.

"O stop! O stop! young man," she said;
  "For I in dule am dight;
O stop, and win a fair lady's luve,
  If you be a leal true knight."

But nothing did the tall knight say,
  And nothing did he blin;
Still slowly rode he on before
  And fast she rade behind.

She whipped her steed, she spurred her steed,
  Till his breast was all a foam;
But nearer unto that tall young knight,
  By Our Ladye she could not come.

"O if you be a gay young knight,
  As well I trow you be,
Pull tight your bridle reins, and stay
  Till I come up to thee."

But nothing did that tall knight say,
  And no whit did he blin,
Until he reached a broad river's side
  And there he drew his rein.

"O is this water deep?" he said,
  "As it is wondrous dun?
Or is it sic as a saikless maid,
  And a leal true knight may swim?"

"The water it is deep," she said,
  "As it is wondrous dun;
But it is sic as a saikless maid,
  And a leal true knight may swim."

The knight spurred on his tall black steed;
  The lady spurred on her brown;
And fast they rade unto the flood,
  And fast they baith swam down.

"The water weets my tae," she said;
  "The water weets my knee,
And hold up my bridle reins, sir knight,
  For the sake of Our Ladye."

"If I would help thee now," he said,
  "It were a deadly sin,
For I've sworn neir to trust a fair may's word,
  Till the water weets her chin."

"Oh, the water weets my waist," she said,
  "Sae does it weet my skin,
And my aching heart rins round about,
  The burn maks sic a din.

"The water is waxing deeper still,
  Sae does it wax mair wide;
And aye the farther that we ride on,
  Farther off is the other side.

"O help me now, thou false, false knight,
  Have pity on my youth,
For now the water jawes owre my head,
  And it gurgles in my mouth."

The knight turned right and round about,
  All in the middle stream;
And he stretched out his head to that lady,
  But loudly she did scream.

"O this is hallow-morn," he said,
  "And it is your bridal-day,
But sad would be that gay wedding,
  If bridegroom and bride were away.

"And ride on, ride on, proud Margaret!
  Till the water comes o'er your bree,
For the bride maun ride deep, and deeper yet,
  Wha rides this ford wi' me.

"Turn round, turn round, proud Margaret!
  Turn ye round, and look on me,
Thou hast killed a true knight under trust,
  And his ghost now links on with thee."

. . . .

ROSE THE RED AND WHITE LILY

(*Child*, Part IV.)

O Rose the Red and White Lilly,
  Their mother dear was dead,
And their father married an ill woman,
  Wishd them twa little guede.

Yet she had twa as fu fair sons
  As eer brake manis bread,
And the tane of them loed her White Lilly,
  And the tither lood Rose the Red.

O, biggit ha they a bigly bowr,
  And strawn it oer wi san,
And there was mair mirth i the ladies' bowr
  Than in a' their father's lan.

But out it spake their step-mother,
  Wha stood a little foreby:
" I hope to live and play the prank
  Sal gar your loud sang ly."

She's calld upon her eldest son:
  " Come here, my son, to me;
It fears me sair, my eldest son,
  That ye maun sail the sea."

" Gin it fear you sair, my mither dear,
  Your bidding I maun dee;
But be never war to Rose the Red
  Than ye ha been to me."

"O had your tongue, my eldest son,
  For sma sal be her part ;
You'll nae get a kiss o her comely mouth
  Gin your very fair heart should break."

She's calld upon her youngest son :
  "Come here, my son, to me ;
It fears me sair, my youngest son,
  That ye maun sail the sea."

"Gin it fear you sair, my mither dear,
  Your bidding I maun dee ;
But be never war to White Lilly
  Than ye ha been to me."

"O haud your tongue, my youngest son,
  For sma sall be her part ;
You'll neer get a kiss o her comely mouth
  Tho your very fair heart should break."

When Rose the Red and White Lilly
  Saw their twa loves were gane,
Then stopped ha they their loud, loud sang,
  And tane up the still moarnin ;
And their step-mother stood listnin by,
  To hear the ladies' mean.

Then out it spake her, White Lily ;
  " My sister, we'll be gane ;
Why shou'd we stay in Barnsdale,
  To waste our youth in pain?"

Then cutted ha they their green cloathing,
  A little below their knee ;
And sae ha they their yallow hair,
  A little aboon there bree ;
And they've doen them to haely chapel
  Was christened by Our Ladye.

There ha they changed their ain twa names,
    Sae far frae ony town;
And the tane o them hight Sweet Willy,
    And the tither o them Roge the Roun.

Between this twa a vow was made,
    An they sware it to fulfil;
That at three blasts o a buglehorn,
    She'd come her sister till.

Now Sweet Willy's gane to the kingis court,
    Her true-love for to see,
And Roge the Roun to good green wood,
    Brown Robin's man to be.

As it fell out upon a day,
    They a did put the stane;
Full seven foot ayont them a
    She gard the puttin-stane gang.

She leand her back against an oak,
    And gae a loud Ohone!
Then out it spake him Brown Robin,
    "But that's a woman's moan!"

"Oh, ken ye by my red rose lip?
    Or by my yallow hair;
Or ken ye by my milk-white breast?
    For ye never saw it bare?"

"I ken no by your red rose lip,
    Nor by your yallow hair;
Nor ken I by your milk-white breast,
    For I never saw it bare;
But, come to your bowr whaever sae likes,
    Will find a ladye there."

"Oh, gin ye come to my bowr within,
   Thro fraud, deceit, or guile,
Wi this same bran that's in my han
   I swear I will thee kill."

"But I will come thy bowr within,
   An spear nae leave," quoth he ;
"An this same bran that's i my han,
   I sall ware back on the."

About the tenth hour of the night,
   The ladie's bowr door was broken,
An eer the first hour of the day
   The bonny knave bairn was gotten.

When days were gane and months were run,
   The ladye took travailing,
And sair she cry'd for a bow'r-woman,
   For to wait her upon.

Then out it spake him, Brown Robin :
   "Now what needs a' this din?
For what coud any woman do
   But I coud do the same?"

"'Twas never my mither's fashion," she says,
   "Nor sall it ever be mine,
That belted knights shoud eer remain
   Where ladies dreed their pine.

"But ye take up that bugle-horn,
   An blaw a blast for me ;
I ha a brother i the kingis court
   Will come me quickly ti."

"O gin ye ha a brither on earth
   That ye love better nor me,
Ye blaw the horn yoursel," he says,
   "For ae blast I winna gie."

She's set the horn till her mouth,
    And she's blawn three blasts sae shrill;
Sweet Willy heard i the kingis court,
    And came her quickly till.

Then up it started Brown Robin,
    An an angry man was he:
"There comes nae man this bowr within
    But first must fight wi me."

O they hae fought that bowr within
    Till the sun was gaing down,
Till drops o blude frae Rose the Red
    Cam trailing to the groun.

She leand her back against the wa,
    Says, "Robin, let a' be;
For it is a lady born and bred
    That's foughten sae well wi thee."

O seven foot he lap a back;
    Says, "Alas, and wae is me!
I never wisht in a' my life,
    A woman's blude to see;
An ae for the sake of ae fair maid
    Whose name was White Lilly."

Then out it spake her White Lilly,
    An a hearty laugh laugh she:
"She's lived wi you this year an mair,
    Tho ye kenntna it was she."

Now word has gane thro a' the lan,
    Before a month was done,
That Brown Robin's man, in good green wood,
    Had born a bonny young son.

The word has gane to the kingis court,
   An to the king himsel;
"Now, by my fay," the king could say,
   "The like was never heard tell!"

Then out it spake him Bold Arthur,
   An a hearty laugh laugh he:
"I trow some may has playd the loun,
   And fled her ain country."

"Bring me my steed," then cry'd the king,
   "My bow and arrows keen;
I'll ride mysel to good green wood,
   An see what's to be seen."

"An't please your grace," said Bold Arthur,
   "My liege, I'll gang you wi,
An try to fin a little foot-page,
   That's strayd awa frae me."

O they've hunted i the good green wood
   The buck but an the rae,
An they drew near Brown Robin's bowr,
   About the close of day.

Then out it spake the king in hast,
   Says, "Arthur look an see
Gin that be no your little foot-page
   That leans against yon tree."

Then Arthur took his bugle-horn,
   An blew a blast sae shrill;
Sweet Willy started at the sound,
   An ran him quickly till.

"O wanted ye your meat, Willy?
   Or wanted ye your fee?
Or gat ye ever an angry word,
   That ye ran awa frae me?"

"I wanted nought, my master dear;
  To me ye ay was good;
I came but to see my ae brother,
  That wons in this green wood."

Then out it spake the king again,
  Says, "Bonny boy, tell to me,
Wha lives into yon bigly bowr,
  Stands by yon green oak tree?"

"Oh, pardon me," says Sweet Willie,
  "My liege, I dare no tell;
An I pray you go no near that bowr,
  For fear they do you fell."

"Oh, haud your tongue, my bonny boy,
  For I winna be said nay;
But I will gang that bowr within,
  Betide me weal or wae."

They've lighted off their milk-white steeds,
  An saftly enterd in,
And there they saw her White Lilly,
  Nursing her bonny young son.

"Now, by the rood," the king coud say,
  "This is a comely sight;
I trow, instead of a forrester's man,
  This is a lady bright!"

Then out it spake her, Rose the Red,
  An fell low down on her knee:
"Oh, pardon us, my gracious liege,
  An our story I'll tell thee.

"Our father was a wealthy lord,
  That wond in Barnsdale;
But we had a wicked step-mother,
  That wrought us meickle bale.

"Yet she had twa as fu fair sons
   As ever the sun did see,
An the tane of them lood my sister dear,
   An the tother said he lood me."

Then out it spake him Bold Arthur,
   As by the king he stood :
"Now, by the faith o my body,
   This shoud be Rose the Red ! "

Then in it came him Brown Robin,
   Frae hunting o the deer ;
But whan he saw the king was there,
   He started back for fear.

The king has taen him by the hand,
   An bade him naithing dread ;
Says, " Ye maun leave the good greenwood,
   Come to the court wi speed."

Then up he took White Lilly's son,
   An set him on his knee ;
Says—" Gin ye live to wield a bran,
   My bowman ye sall bee."

The king he sent for robes of green,
   An girdles o shinning gold ;
He gart the ladies be arrayd
   Most comely to behold.

They've done them unto Mary kirk,
   An there gat fair wedding,
An fan the news spread oer the lan,
   For joy the bells did ring.

Then out it spake her Rose the Red,
   An a hearty laugh laugh she :
"I wonder what would our step-dame say,
   Gin she his sight did see ! "

THE BATTLE OF HARLAW

EVERGREEN VERSION

(Child, vol. vii. Early Edition, Appendix.)

FRAE Dunidier as I cam throuch,
  Doun by the hill of Banochie,
Allangst the lands of Garioch.
  Grit pitie was to heir and se
  The noys and dulesum hermonie,
That evir that dreiry day did daw!
  Cryand the corynoch on hie,
Alas! alas! for the Harlaw.

I marvlit what the matter meant;
  All folks were in a fiery fariy:
  wist nocht wha was fae or freind,
  Yet quietly I did me carrie.
  But sen the days of auld King Hairy,
Sic slauchter was not hard nor sene,
  And thair I had nae tyme to tairy,
For bissiness in Aberdene.

Thus as I walkit on the way,
  To Inverury as I went,
I met a man, and bad him stay,
  Requeisting him to mak me quaint
  Of the beginning and the event
That happenit thair at the Harlaw;
  Then he entreited me to tak tent,
And he the truth sould to me schaw.

Grit Donald of the Ysles did claim
  Unto the lands of Ross sum richt,
And to the governour he came,
  Them for to haif, gif that he micht,
  Wha saw his interest was but slicht,
And thairfore answerit with disdain.
  He hastit hame baith day and nicht,
And sent nae bodward back again.

But Donald richt impatient
  Of that answer Duke Robert gaif,
He vow'd to God Omniyotent,
  All the hale lands of Ross to haif,
  Or ells be graithed in his graif:
He wald not quat his richt for nocht,
  Nor be abusit like a slaif;
That bargin sould be deirly bocht.

Then haistylie he did command
  That all his weir-men should convene;
Ilk an well harnisit frae hand,
  To meit and heir what he did mein.
  He waxit wrath and vowit tein;
Sweirand he wald surpryse the North,
  Subdew the brugh of Aberdene,
Mearns, Angus, and all Fyfe to Forth.

Thus with the weir-men of the yles,
  Wha war ay at his bidding bown,
With money maid, with forss and wyls,
  Richt far and neir, baith up and doun,
  Throw mount and muir, frae town to town,
Allangst the lands of Ross he roars,
  And all obey'd at his bandown,
Evin frae the North to Suthren shoars.

Then all the countrie men did yield;
  For nae resistans durst they mak,

Nor offer batill in the feild,
   Be forss of arms to beir him bak.
  Syne they resolvit all and spak,
That best it was for thair behoif,
   They sould him for thair chiftain tak,
Believing weil he did them luve.

Then he a proclamation maid,
   All men to meet at Inverness,
Throw Murray land to mak a raid,
   Frae Arthursyre unto Spey-ness.
   And further mair, he sent express,
To schaw his collours and ensenzie,
   To all and sindry, mair and less,
Throchout the bounds of Byne and Enzie.

And then throw fair Strathbogie land
   His purpose was for to pursew,
And whatsoevir durst gainstand,
   That race they should full sairly rew.
   Then he bad all his men be trew,
And him defend by forss and slicht,
   And promist them rewardis anew,
And mak them men of mekle micht.

Without resistans, as he said,
   Throw all these parts he stoutly past,
Where sum war wae, and sum war glaid,
   But Garioch was all agast.
   Throw all these feilds he sped him fast,
For sic a sicht was never sene;
   And then, forsuith, he langd at last
To se the bruch of Aberdene.

To hinder this prowd enterprise,
   The stout and michty Erl of Marr
With all his men in arms did ryse,
   Even frae **Curgarf** to **Craigyvar**:

And down the syde of Don richt far,
Angus and Mearns did all convene
   To fecht, or Donald came sae nar
The ryall bruch of Aberdene.

And thus the martial Erle of Marr
   Marcht with his men in richt array;
Befoir his enemis was aware,
   His banner bauldly did display.
   For weil enewch they kent the way,
And all their semblance weil they saw:
   Without all dangir or delay,
Come haistily to the Harlaw.

With him the braif Lord Ogilvy,
   Of Angus sheriff principall,
The constable of gude Dundè,
   The vanguard led before them all.
   Suppose in number they war small,
Thay first richt bauldlie did pursew,
   And maid thair faes befor them fall,
Wha then that race did sairly rew.

And then the worthy Lord Salton,
   The strong undoubted Laird of Drum,
The stalwart Laird of Lawristone,
   With ilk thair forces all and sum.
   Panmuir with all his men, did cum,
The provost of braif Aberdene,
   With trumpets and with tuick of drum,
Came schortly in thair armour schene.

These with the Earle of Marr came on,
   In the reir-ward richt orderlie,
Thair enemies to sett upon;
   In awfull manner hardilie,
   Togither vowit to live and die,
Since they had marchit mony mylis,
   For to suppress the tyrannie
Of douted Donald of the Ysles.

But he, in number ten to ane,
   Right subtilè alang did ryde,
With Malcomtosch, and feil Maclean,
   With all thair power at thair syde;
   Presumeand on their strenth and pryde,
Without all feir or ony aw,
   Richt bauldie battil did abyde,
Hard by the town of fair Harlaw.

The armies met, the trumpet sounds,
   The dandring drums alloud did touk,
Baith armies byding on the bounds,
   Till ane of them the feild sould bruik.
   Nae help was thairfor, nane wald jouk,
Ferss was the fecht on ilka syde,
   And on the ground lay mony a bouk
Of them that thair did battil byd.

With doutsum victorie they dealt,
   The bludy battil lastit lang;
Each man his nibours forss thair felt,
   The weakest aft-tymes gat the wrang:
   Thair was nae mowis thair them amang,
Naithing was hard but heavy knocks,
   That eccho mad a dulefull sang,
Thairto resounding frae the rocks.

But Donalds men at last gaif back,
   For they war all out of array:
The Earl of Marris men throw them brak,
   Pursewing shairply in thair way,
   Thair enemys to tak or slay,
Be dynt of forss to gar them yield;
   Wha war richt blyth to win away,
And sae for feirdness tint the feild.

Then Donald fled, and that full fast,
   To mountains hich for all his micht;
For he and his war all agast,
   And ran till they war out of sicht;

And sae of Ross he lost his richt,
Thocht mony men with hem he brocht;
   Towards the yles fled day and nicht,
And all he wan was deirlie bocht.

This is (quod he) the richt report
   Of all that I did heir and knaw;
Thocht my discourse be sumthing schort,
   Tak this to be a richt suthe saw:
   Contrairie God and the kings law,
Thair was spilt mekle Christian blude,
   Into the battil of Harlaw:
This is the sum, sae I conclude.

But yet a bonnie while abide,
   And I sall mak thee cleirly ken
What slauchter was on ilkay syde,
   Of Lowland and of Highland men,
   Wha for thair awin haif evir bene;
These lazie lowns micht weil be spared,
   Chased like deers into their dens,
And gat their wages for reward.

Malcomtosh, of the clan heid-cheif,
   Macklean with his grit hauchty heid,
With all thair succour and relief,
   War dulefully dung to the deid;
   And now we are freid of thair feid,
They will not lang to cum again;
   Thousands with them, without remeid,
On Donald's syd, that day war slain.

And on the uther syde war lost,
   Into the feild that dismal day,
Chief men of worth, of mekle cost,
   To be lamentit sair for ay.
   The Lord Saltoun of Rothemay,
A man of micht and mekle main;
   Grit dolour was for his decay,
That sae unhappylie was slain.

Of the best men amang them was
   The gracious gude Lord Ogilvy,
The sheriff-principal of Angus,
   Renownit for truth and equitie,
   For faith and magnanimitie;
He had few fallows in the field,
   Yet fell by fatall destinie,
For he naeways wad grant to yield.

Sir James Scrimgeor of Duddap, knicht,
   Grit constabill of fair Dundè,
Unto the dulefull deith was dicht;
   The kingis cheif bannerman was he,
   A valiant man of chevalrie,
Whose predecessors wan that place
   At Spey, with gude King William frie
'Gainst Murray, and Macduncan's race.

Gude Sir Allexander Irving,
   The much renowit laird of Drum,
Nane in his days was bettir sene
   When they war semblit all and sum.
   To praise him we sould not be dumm,
For valour, witt, and worthyness;
   To end his days he ther did cum
Whose ransom is remeidyless.

And thair the knicht of Lawriston
   Was slain into his armour schene,
And gude Sir Robert Davidson,
   Wha provost was of Aberdene:
   The knicht of Panmure, as was sene,
A mortall man in armour bricht,
   Sir Thomas Murray, stout and kene,
Left to the warld thair last gude nicht.

Thair was not sen King Keneths days
   Sic strange intestine crewel stryf
In Scotland sene, as ilk man says,
   Whare mony liklie lost thair lyfe;

Whilk maid divorce twene man and wyfe,
And mony childrene fatherless,
　Whilk in this realme has bene full ryfe:
Lord help these lands, our wrangs redress.

In July, on Saint James his even,
　That four and twenty dismall day,
Twelve hundred, ten score and eleven
　Of theirs sen Chryst, the suthe to say,
　Men will remember, as they may,
When thus the ventie they knaw,
　And mony a ane may murn for ay,
The brim battil of the Harlaw.

―◇―

Traditionary Version

(*Child*, Part VI.)

As I came in by Dunidier,
　An doun by Netherha,
There was fifty thousand Hielanmen
　A marching to Harlaw.
(*Chorus*) Wi a dree dree dradie drumtie dree.

As I cam on, an farther on,
　An doun an by Balquhain,
Oh there I met Sir James the Rose,
　Wi him Sir John the Gryme.

"O cam ye frae the Hielans, man?
　And cam ye a' the wey?
Saw ye Macdonell an his men,
　As they cam frae the Skee?"

"Yes, me cam frae ta Hielans, man,
　An me cam a ta wey,
An she saw Macdonell an his men,
　As they cam frae ta Skee."

"Oh, was ye near Macdonell's men?
  Did ye their numbers see?
Come, tell to me, John Hielanman,
  What micht their numbers be?"

"Yes, me was near, an near eneuch,
  An me their numbers saw;
There was fifty thousand Hielanmen
  A marching to Harlaw."

"Gin that be true," says James the Rose,
  "We'll no come meikle speed;
We'll cry upo our merry men,
  And lichtly mount our steed."

"Oh no, oh no!" quo' John the Gryme,
  "That thing maun never be;
The gallant Grymes were never bate,
  We'll try what we can dee."

As I cam on, an farther on,
  An doun an by Harlaw,
They fell fu close on ilka side;
  Sic fun ye never saw.

They fell fu close on ilka side,
  Sic fun ye never saw;
For Hielan swords gied clash for clash,
  At the battle o Harlaw.

The Hielanmen, wi their lang swords,
  They laid on us fu sair,
An they drave back our merry men
  Three acres breadth an mair.

Brave Forbës to his brither did say,
  "Noo brither, dinna ye see?
They beat us back on ilka side,
  An we'se be forced to flee."

"Oh no, oh no, my brither dear,
　That thing maun never be;
Tak ye your good sword in your hand,
　An come your wa's wi me."

"Oh no, oh no, my brither dear,
　The clans they are ower strang,
An they drive back our merry men,
　Wi swords baith sharp an lang."

Brave Forbës drew his men aside,
　Said, "Tak your rest a while,
Until I to Drumminnor send,
　To fess my coat o mail."

The servan he did ride,
　An his horse it did na fail,
For in twa hours an a quarter
　He brocht the coat o mail.

Then back to back the brithers twa
　Gaed in amo the thrang,
An they hewed doun the Hielanmen,
　Wi swords baith sharp an lang.

Macdonell he was young an stout,
　Had on his coat o mail,
And he has gane oot throw them a'
　To try his han himsell.

The first ae straik that Forbës strack,
　He garrt Macdonell reel;
An the neist ae straik that Forbës strack,
　The great Macdonell fell.

And siccan a lierachie,
　I'm sure ye never sawe
As wis amo the Hielanmen,
　When they saw Macdonell fa.

An whan they saw that he was deid,
   They turnd and ran awa,
An they buried him in Legget's Den,
   A large mile frae Harlaw.

They rade, they ran, an some did gang,
   They were o sma record ;
But Forbës and his merry men,
   They slew them a' the road.

On Monanday, at mornin,
   The battle it began,
On Saturday at gloamin',
   Ye'd scarce kent wha had wan.

An sic a weary buryin,
   I'm sure ye never saw,
As wis the Sunday after that,
   On the muirs aneath Harlaw.

Gin anybody speer at ye
   For them ye took awa,
Ye may tell their wives and bairnies,
   They're sleepin at Harlaw.

DICKIE MACPHALION

(Sharpe's *Ballad Book*, No. XIV.)

I WENT to the mill, but the miller was gone,
I sat me down, and cried ochone !
To think on the days that are past and gone,
  Of Dickie Macphalion that's slain.
    Shoo, shoo, shoolaroo,
To think on the days that are past and gone,
  Of Dickie Macphalion that's slain.

I sold my rock, I sold my reel,
And sae hae I my spinning wheel,
And a' to buy a cap of steel
  For Dickie Macphalion that's slain !
    Shoo, shoo, shoolaroo,
And a' to buy a cap of steel
  For Dickie Macphalion that's slain.

A LYKE-WAKE DIRGE

(*Border Minstrelsy*, vol. ii., p. 357.)

This ae nighte, this ae nighte,
   Every nighte and alle,
Fire, and sleet, and candle-lighte,
   And Christe receive thye saule.

When thou from hence away art paste,
   Every nighte and alle,
To Whinny-muir thou comest at laste;
   And Christe receive thye saule.

If ever thou gavest hosen and shoon,
   Every nighte and alle,
Sit thee down and put them on;
   And Christe receive thye saule.

If hosen and shoon thou ne'er gavest nane,
   Every nighte and alle,
The whinnes sall pricke thee to the bare bane;
   And Christe receive thye saule.

From Whinny-muir when thou mayst passe,
   Every nighte and alle,
To Brigg o' Dread thou comest at laste,
   And Christe receive thye saule.

   ·   ·   ·   ·   ·

From Brigg o' Dread when thou mayst passe,
   Every nighte and alle,
To Purgatory fire thou comest at last,
   And Christe receive thye saule.

If ever thou gavest meat or drink,
   Every nighte and alle,
The fire sall never make thee shrinke;
   And Christe receive thye saule.

If meate or drinke thou never gavest nane,
   Every nighte and alle,
The fire will burn thee to the bare bane;
   And Christe receive thye saule.

This ae nighte, this ae nighte,
   Every nighte and alle,
Fire, and sleet, and candle-lighte,
   And Christe receive thye saule.

THE LAIRD OF WARISTOUN

(Child, vol. iii.   Early Edition.)

Down by yon garden green,
  Sae merrily as she gaes;
She has twa weel-made feet,
  And she trips upon her taes.

She has twa weel-made feet;
  Far better is her hand;
She's as jimp in the middle
  As ony willow wand.

" Gif ye will do my bidding,
  At my bidding for to be,
It's I will make you lady
  Of a' the lands you see."

.   .   .   .   .

He spak a word in jest;
  Her answer was na good;
He threw a plate at her face,
  Made it a' gush out o' blood.

She wasna frae her chamber
  A step but barely three,
When up and at her richt hand
  There stood Man's Enemy.

" Gif ye will do my bidding,
  At my bidding for to be,
I'll learn you a wile,
  Avenged for to be."

The foul thief knotted the tether;
   She lifted his head on hie;
The nourice drew the knot
   That gar'd lord Waristoun die.

Then word is gane to Leith,
   Also to Edinburgh town
That the lady had kill'd the laird,
   The laird o' Waristoun.

. . . . .

Tak aff, tak aff my hood
   But lat my petticoat be;
Put my mantle o'er my head;
   For the fire I downa see.

Now, a' ye gentle maids,
   Tak warning now by me,
And never marry ane
   But wha pleases your e'e.

"For he married me for love,
   But I married him for fee;
And sae brak out the feud
   That gar'd my dearie die."

MAY COLVEN

(*Child*, Part I., p. 56.)

False Sir John a wooing came
  To a maid of beauty fair;
May Colven was this lady's name,
  Her father's only heir.

He wood her butt, he wood her ben,
  He wood her in the ha,
Until he got this lady's consent
  To mount and ride awa.

He went down to her father's bower,
  Where all the steeds did stand,
And he's taken one of the best steeds
  That was in her father's land.

He's got on and she's got on,
  As fast as they could flee,
Until they came to a lonesome part,
  A rock by the side of the sea.

"Loup off the steed," says false Sir John,
  "Your bridal bed you see;
For I have drowned seven young ladies,
  The eighth one you shall be.

"Cast off, cast off, my May Colven,
  All and your silken gown,
For it's oer good and oer costly
  To rot in the salt sea foam.

"Cast off, cast off, my May Colven,
 All and your embroiderd shoen,
For they're oer good and oer costly
 To rot in the salt sea foam."

"O turn you about, O false Sir John,
 And look to the leaf of the tree,
For it never became a gentleman
 A naked woman to see."

He turned himself straight round about,
 To look to the leaf of the tree,
So swift as May Colven was
 To throw him in the sea.

"O help, O help, my May Colven,
 O help, or else I'll drown;
I'll take you home to your father's bower,
 And set you down safe and sound."

"No help, no help, O false Sir John,
 No help, nor pity thee;
Tho' seven kings' daughters you have drownd,
 But the eighth shall not be me."

So she went on her father's steed,
 As swift as she could flee,
And she came home to her father's bower
 Before it was break of day.

Up then and spoke the pretty parrot:
 "May Colven, where have you been?
What has become of false Sir John,
 That woo'd you so late the streen?

"He woo'd you butt, he woo'd you ben,
 He woo'd you in the ha,
Until he got your own consent
 For to mount and gang awa."

"O hold your tongue, my pretty parrot,
   Lay not the blame upon me;
Your cup shall be of the flowered gold,
   Your cage of the root of the tree."

Up then spake the king himself,
   In the bed-chamber where he lay:
"What ails the pretty parrot,
   That prattles so long or day?"

"There came a cat to my cage door,
   It almost a worried me,
And I was calling on May Colven
   To take the cat from me."

JOHNIE FAA

(*Child*, vol. iv. Early Edition.)

The gypsies came to our good lord's gate
   And wow but they sang sweetly!
They sang sae sweet and sae very complete
   That down came the fair lady.

And she came tripping doun the stair,
   And a' her maids before her;
As soon as they saw her weel-far'd face,
   They coost the glamer o'er her.

"O come with me," says Johnie Faw,
   "O come with me, my dearie;
For I vow and I swear by the hilt of my sword,
   That your lord shall nae mair come near ye."

Then she gied them the beer and the wine,
   And they gied her the ginger;
But she gied them a far better thing,
   The goud ring aff her finger.

"Gae take frae me this yay mantle,
   And bring to me a plaidie;
For if kith and kin, and a' had sworn,
   I'll follow the gypsy laddie.

"Yestreen I lay in a weel-made bed,
  Wi' my good lord beside me;
But this night I'll lye in a tenant's barn,
  Whatever shall betide me!"

"Come to your bed," says Johnie Faw,
  "Oh, come to your bed, my dearie:
For I vow and swear by the hilt of my sword,
  Your lord shall nae mair come near ye."

"I'll go to bed to my Johnie Faw,
  I'll go to bed to my dearie;
For I vow and I swear by the fan in my hand,
  My lord shall nae mair come near me.

"I'll mak a hap to my Johnie Faw,
  I'll mak a hap to my dearie;
And he's get a' the coat gaes round,
  And my lord shall nae mair come near me."

And when our lord came hame at e'en,
  And spier'd for his fair lady,
The tane she cry'd, and the other reply'd,
  "She's awa' wi' the gypsy laddie!"

"Gae saddle to me the black black steed,
  Gae saddle and make him ready;
Before that I either eat or sleep,
  I'll gae seek my fair lady."

And we were fifteen weel-made men,
  Altho' we were na bonny;
And we were a' put down but ane,
  For a fair young wanton lady.

HOBBIE NOBLE

(*Child*, vi. Early Edition.)

FOUL fa' the breast first treason bred in !
    That Liddesdale may safely say :
For in it there was baith meat and drink,
    And corn unto our geldings gay.

We were stout-hearted men and true,
    As England it did often say ;
But now we may turn our backs and fly,
    Since brave Noble is seld away.

Now Hobie he was an English man,
    And born into Bewcastle dale ;
But his misdeeds they were sae great,
    They banish'd him to Liddisdale.

At Kershope foot the tryst was set,
    Kershope of the lilye lee ;
And there was traitour Sim o' the Mains,
    With him a private companie.

Then Hobie has graith'd his body weel,
    I wat it was wi' baith good iron and steel ;
And he has pull'd out his fringed grey,
    And there, brave Noble, he rade him weel.

Then Hobie is down the water gane,
    E'en as fast as he may drie;
'Tho' they shoud a' brusten and broken their
      hearts,
    Frae that tryst Noble he would na be.

"Weel may ye be, my feiries five!
    And aye, what is your wills wi' me?"
Then they cry'd a' wi' ae consent,
    "Thou'rt welcome here, brave Noble, to
      me.

"Wilt thou with us in England ride,
    And thy safe warrand we will be?
If we get a horse worth a hundred punds,
    Upon his back that thou shalt be."

"I dare not with you into England ride;
    The Land-sergeant has me at feid:
I know not what evil may betide,
    For Peter of Whitfield, his brother, is
      dead.

"And Anton Shiel he loves not me,
    For I gat twa drifts o his sheep;
The great Earl of Whitfield loves me not,
    For nae gear frae me he e'er could keep.

"But will ye stay till the day gae down,
    Until the night come o'er the grund,
And I'll be a guide worth ony twa,
    That may in Liddesdale be fund?

"Tho' dark the night as pitch and tar,
    I'll guide ye o'er yon hills fu' hie;
And bring ye a' in safety back,
    If ye'll be true and follow me."

He's guided them o'er moss and muir,
    O'er hill and houp, and mony a down ;
Til they came to the Foulbogshiel,
    And there, brave Noble, he lighted down.

But word is gane to the Land-sergeant,
    In Askirton where that he lay—
"The deer that ye hae hunted lang,
    Is seen into the Waste this day."

"Then Hobbie Noble is that deer !
    I wat he carries the style fu' hie ;
Aft has he beat your slough-hounds back,
    And set yourselves at little lee.

"Gar warn the bows of Hartlie-burn ;
    See they shaft their arrows on the wa' !
Warn Willeva and Spear Edom,
    And see the morn they meet me a'.

"Gar meet me on the Rodric-haugh,
    And see it be by break o' day ;
And we will on to Conscowthart-Green,
    For there, I think, we'll get our prey."

Then Hobbie Noble has dream'd a dream,
    In the Foulbogshiel, where that he lay ;
He thought his horse was neath him shot,
    And he himself got hard away.

The cocks could crow, the day could dawn,
    And I wot so even down fell the rain ;
If Hobbie had no waken'd at that time,
    In the Foulbogshiel he had been tane or slain.

"Get up, get up, my feiries five !
    For I wot here makes a fu' ill day ;
Yet the warst cloak of this companie,
    I hope, shall cross the Waste this day."

Now Hobie thought the gates were clear;
    But, ever alas! it was not sae:
They were beset wi' cruel men and keen,
    That away brave Hobbie could not gae.

"Yet follow me, my feiries five,
    And see of me ye keep good ray;
And the worst cloak o' this companie
    I hope shall cross the Waste this day."

There was heaps of men now Hobbie before,
    And other heaps was him behind,
That had he wight as Wallace was,
    Away brave Noble he could not win.

Then Hobie he had but a laddies sword;
    But he did more than a laddies deed;
In the midst of Conscouthart-Green,
    He brake it oer Jersawigham's head.

Now they have tane brave Hobie Noble,
    Wi' his ain bowstring they band him sae;
And I wat heart was ne'er sae sair,
    As when his ain five band him on the brae.

They have tane him on for West Carlisle;
    They ask'd him if he knew the way?
Whate'er he thought, yet little he said;
    He knew the way as well as they.

They hae ta'en him up the Ricker gate;
    The wives they cast their windows wide;
And every wife to anither can say,
    "That's the man loos'd Jock o' the Side!"

"Fye on ye, women! why ca' ye me man?
    For it's nae man that I'm used like;
I am but like a forfoughen hound,
    Has been fighting in a dirty syke."

Then they hae tane him up thro' Carlisle
    town,
  And set him by the chimney fire;
They gave brave Noble a wheat loaf to eat,
  And that was little his desire.

Then they gave him a wheat loaf to eat,
  And after that a can o beer;
Then they cried a' with ae consent,
  "Eat, brave Noble, and make gude cheer!

"Confess my lord's horse, Hobie," they
    said,
  "And the morn in Carlisle thou's no
    die;"
"How shall I confess them," Hobie says,
  "For I never saw them with mine eye?"

Then Hobie has sworn a fu' great aith,
  By the day that he was gotten and born,
He never had ony thing o' my lord's,
  That either eat him grass or corn.

"Now fare thee weel, sweet Mangerton!
  For I think again I'll ne'er thee see:
I wad betray nae lad alive,
  For a' the goud in Christentie.

"And fare thee weel, sweet Liddesdale!
  Baith the hie land and the law;
Keep ye weel frae traitor Mains!
  For goud and gear he'll sell ye a'.

"Yet wad I rather be ca'd Hobie Noble,
  In Carlisle where he suffers for his faut,
Before I'd be ca'd traitor Mains,
  That eats and drinks of the meal and
    maut."

THE TWA SISTERS

(Sharpe's *Ballad Book*, No. X., p. 30.)

There liv'd twa sisters in a bower,
  Hey Edinbruch, how Edinbruch.
There liv'd twa sisters in a bower,
    Stirling for aye :
The youngest o' them, O, she was a flower !
Bonny Sanct Johnstonne that stands upon Tay.

There came a squire frae the west,
  Hey Edinbruch, how Edinbruch.
There cam a squire frae the west,
    Stirling for aye :
He lo'ed them baith, but the youngest best,
Bonny Sanct Johnstonne that stands upon Tay.

He gied the eldest a gay gold ring,
  Hey Edinbruch, how Edinbruch.
He gied the eldest a gay gold ring,
    Stirling for aye :
But he lo'ed the youngest aboon a' thing,
Bonny Sanct Johnstonne that stands upon Tay.

"Oh sister, sister, will ye go to the sea?
   Hey Edinbruch, how Edinbruch.
Oh sister, sister, will ye go to the sea?
     Stirling for aye:
Our father's ships sail bonnilie,
Bonny Sanct Johnstonne that stands upon
   Tay."

The youngest sat down upon a stane,
   Hey Edinbruch, how Edinbruch.
The youngest sat down upon a stane,
     Stirling for aye:
The eldest shot the youngest in,
Bonny Sanct Johnstonne that stands upon
   Tay.

"Oh sister, sister, lend me your hand,
   Hey Edinbruch, how Edinbruch.
Oh, sister, sister, lend me your hand,
     Stirling for aye:
And you shall hae my gouden fan,
Bonny Sanct Johnstonne that stands upon
   Tay.

"Oh, sister, sister, save my life,
   Hey Edinbruch, how Edinbruch.
Oh sister, sister, save my life,
     Stirling for aye:
And ye shall be the squire's wife,
Bonny Sweet Johnstonne that stands upon
   Tay."

First she sank, and then she swam,
   Hey Edinbruch, how Edinbruch.
First she sank, and then she swam,
     Stirling for aye:
Until she cam to Tweed mill dam,
Bonny Sanct Johnstonne that stands upon
   Tay.

The millar's daughter was baking bread,
  Hey Edinbruch, how Edinbruch.
The millar's daughter was baking bread,
    Stirling for aye:
She went for water, as she had need,
Bonny Sanct Johnstonne that stands upon
    Tay.

"Oh father, father, in our mill dam,
  Hey Edinbruch, how Edinbruch,
Oh father, father, in our mill dam,
    Stirling for aye:
There's either a lady, or a milk-white
    swan,
Bonny Sanct Johnstonne that stands upon
    Tay.

They could nae see her fingers small,
  Hey Edinbruch, how Edinbruch.
They could nae see her fingers small,
    Stirling for aye:
Wi' diamond rings they were cover'd all,
Bonny Sanct Johnstonne that stands upon Tay.

They could nae see her yellow hair,
  Hey Edinbruch, how Edinbruch.
They could nae see her yellow hair,
    Stirling for aye:
Sae mony knots and platts war there,
Bonny Sanct Johnstonne that stands upon
    Tay.

Bye there cam a fiddler fair,
  Hey Edinbruch, how Edinbruch.
Bye there cam a fiddler fair,
    Stirling for aye:
And he's ta'en three tails o' her yellow
    hair,
Bonny Sanct Johnstonne that stands upon
    Tay.

. . . . .

MARY AMBREE

(*Reliques of Ancient English Poetry*, vol. ii. p. 230.)

When captaines couragious, whom death cold not daunte,
Did march to the siege of the city of Gaunt,
They mustred their souldiers by two and by three,
And the formost in battle was Mary Ambree.

When [the] brave sergeant-major was slaine in her sight,
Who was her true lover, her joy, and delight,
Because he was slaine most treacherouslie
Then vowd to revenge him Mary Ambree.

She clothed herselfe from the top to the toe
In buffe of the bravest, most seemelye to showe;
A faire shirt of male then slipped on shee:
Was not this a brave bonny lasse, Mary Ambree?

A helmett of proofe shee strait did provide,
A stronge arminge-sword shee girt by her side,
On her hand a goodly faire gauntlett put shee:
Was not this a brave bonny lasse, Mary Ambree?

Then tooke shee her sworde and her targett
   in hand,
Bidding all such, as wold, [to] bee of her band;
To wayte on her person came thousand and
   three:
Was not this a brave bonny lasse, Mary
   Ambree?

"My soldiers," she saith, "soe valliant and
   bold,
Nowe followe your captaine, whom you doe
   beholde;
Still formost in battell myselfe will I bee:"
Was not this a brave bonny lasse, Mary
   Ambree?

Then cryed out her souldiers, and loude they
   did say,
"Soe well thou becomest this gallant array,
Thy harte and thy weapons so well do agree,
No mayden was ever like Mary Ambree."

She cheared her souldiers, that foughten for
   life,
With ancyent and standard, with drum and
   with fife,
With brave clanging trumpetts, that sounded
   so free;
Was not this a brave bonny lasse, Mary
   Ambree?

"Before I will see the worst of you all
To come into danger of death or of thrall,
This hand and this life I will venture so free:"
Was not this a brave bonny lasse, Mary
   Ambree?

Shee ledd upp her souldiers in battaile array,
Gainst three times theyr number by breake of
the daye;
Seven howers in skirmish continued shee:
Was not this a brave bonny lasse, Mary
Ambree?

She filled the skyes with the smoke of her shott,
And her enemyes bodyes with bulletts so hott;
For one of her own men a score killed shee:
Was not this a brave bonny lasse, Mary
Ambree?

And when her false gunner, to spoyle her
intent,
Away all her pellets and powder had sent,
Straight with her keen weapon she slasht him
in three:
Was not this a brave bonny lasse, Mary
Ambree?

Being falselye betrayed for lucre of hyre,
At length she was forced to make a retyre;
Then her souldiers into a strong castle drew
shee:
Was not this a brave bonny lasse, Mary
Ambree?

Her foes they besett her on everye side,
As thinking close siege shee cold never abide;
To beate down the walles they all did decree:
But stoutlye deffyd them brave Mary Ambree.

Then tooke shee her sword and her targett in
hand,
And mounting the walls all undaunted did
stand,
There daring their captaines to match any
three:
O what a brave captaine was Mary Ambree!

"Now saye, English captaine, what woldest thou give
To ransome thy selfe, which else must not live?
Come yield thy selfe quicklye, or slaine thou must bee:"
Then smiled sweetlye brave Mary Ambree.

"Ye captaines couragious, of valour so bold,
Whom thinke you before you now you doe behold?"
"A knight, sir, of England, and captaine soe free,
Who shortlye with us a prisoner must bee."

"No captaine of England; behold in your sight
Two brests in my bosome, and therefore no knight:
Noe knight, sirs, of England, nor captaine you see,
But a poor simple mayden called Mary Ambree."

"But art thou a woman, as thou dost declare,
Whose valor hath proved so undaunted in warre?
If England doth yield such brave maydens as thee,
Full well may they conquer, faire Mary Ambree."

The Prince of Great Parma heard of her renowne,
Who long had advanced for England's fair crowne;
Hee wooed her and sued her his mistress to bee,
And offered rich presents to Mary Ambree.

But this virtuous mayden despised them all:
"'Ile nere sell my honour for purple nor pall;
A maiden of England, sir, never will bee
The wench of a monarcke," quoth Mary Ambree.

Then to her owne country shee back did returne,
Still holding the foes of faire England in scorne!
Therfore English captaines of every degree
Sing forth the brave valours of Mary Ambree.

ALISON GROSS

O Alison Gross, that lives in yon tow'r,
  The ugliest witch in the north countrie,
She trysted me ae day up till her bow'r,
  And mony fair speeches she made to me.

She straik'd my head, and she kaim'd my hair,
  And she set me down saftly on her knee;
Says—"If ye will be my leman sae true,
  Sae mony braw things as I will you gi'e."

She shaw'd me a mantle of red scarlet,
  With gowden flowers and fringes fine;
Says—"If ye will be my leman sae true,
  This goodly gift it shall be thine."

"Awa, awa, ye ugly witch,
  Haud far awa, and let me be;
I never will be your leman sae true,
  And I wish I were out of your company."

She neist brocht a sark of the saftest silk,
  Weel wrought with pearls about the band;
Says—"If ye will be my ain true love,
  This goodly gift ye shall command."

She show'd me a cup of the good red gowd,
  Weel set with jewels sae fair to see;
Says—"If ye will be my leman sae true,
  This goodly gift I will you gi'e."

"Awa, awa, ye ugly witch,
    Haud far awa, and let me be;
For I wadna ance kiss your ugly mouth,
    For all the gifts that ye cou'd gi'e."

She's turn'd her richt and round about,
    And thrice she blew on a grass-green horn;
And she sware by the moon and the stars aboon,
    That she'd gar me rue the day I was born.

Then out has she ta'en a silver wand,
    And she turn'd her three times round and round;
She mutter'd sic words, that my strength it fail'd,
    And I fell down senseless on the ground.

She turn'd me into an ugly worm,
    And gar'd me toddle about the tree;
And aye on ilka Saturday night,
    Auld Alison Gross she came to me,

With silver basin, and silver kame,
    To kame my headie upon her knee;
But rather than kiss her ugly mouth,
    I'd ha'e toddled for ever about the tree.

But as it fell out on last Hallow-e'en,
    When the seely court was ridin' by,
The queen lighted down on a gowan bank,
    Near by the tree where I wont to lye.

She took me up in her milk-white hand,
    And she straik'd me three times o'er her knee;
She chang'd me again to my ain proper shape,
    And nae mair do I toddle about the tree.

THE HEIR OF LYNNE

OF all the lords in faire Scotland
   A song I will begin :
Amongst them all dwelled a lord
   Which was the unthrifty Lord of Lynne.

His father and mother were dead him froe,
   And so was the head of all his kinne ;
He did neither cease nor blinne
   To the cards and dice that he did run.

To drinke the wine that was so cleere !
   With every man he would make merry.
And then bespake him John of the Scales,
   Unto the heire of Lynne say'd hee,

Sayes "how dost thou, Lord of Lynne,
   Doest either want gold or fee?
Wilt thou not sell thy land so brode
   To such a good fellow as me?

"For . . I . . " he said,
   "My land, take it unto thee ;
I draw you to record, my lords all ; "
   With that he cast him a Gods pennie.

He told him the gold upon the bord,
   It wanted never a bare penny.
"That gold is thine, the land is mine,
   The heire of Lynne I will bee."

"Heeres gold enough," saithe the heire of Lynne,
  "Both for me and my company."
He drunke the wine that was so cleere,
  And with every man he made merry.

Within three quarters of a yeare
  His gold and fee it waxed thinne,
His merry men were from him gone,
  And left himselfe all alone.

He had never a penny left in his purse,
  Never a penny but three,
And one was brasse and another was lead
  And another was white mony.

"Now well-a-day!" said the heire of Lynne,
  "Now well-a-day, and woe is mee!
For when I was the Lord of Lynne,
  I neither wanted gold nor fee;

"For I have sold my lands so broad,
  And have not left me one penny!
I must go now and take some read
  Unto Edenborrow and beg my bread."

He had not beene in Edenborrow
  Nor three quarters of a yeare,
But some did give him and some said nay,
  And some bid "to the deele gang yee!

"For if we should hang some land selfeer,
  The first we would begin with thee."
"Now well-a-day!" said the heire of Lynne,
  "Now well-a-day, and woe is mee!

"For now I have sold my lands so broad
   That merry man is irke with mee;
But when that I was the Lord of Lynne
   Then on my land I lived merrily;

"And now I have sold my land so broade
   That I have not left me one pennye!
God be with my father!" he said,
   "On his land he lived merrily."

Still in a study there as he stood,
   He unbethought him of a bill,
He unbethought him of a bill
   Which his father had left with him.

Bade him he should never on it looke
   Till he was in extreame neede,
"And by my faith," said the heire of Lynne,
   "Then now I had never more neede."

He tooke the bill and looked it on,
   Good comfort that he found there;
It told him of a castle wall
   Where there stood three chests in feare:

Two were full of the beaten gold,
The third was full of white money.
He turned then downe his bags of bread
And filled them full of gold so red.

Then he did never cease nor blinne
Till John of the Scales house he did winne.
When that he came John of the Scales,
Up at the speere he looked then;

There sate three lords upon a rowe,
  And John o' the Scales sate at the bord's head,
And John o' the Scales sate at the bord's head
Because he was the lord of Lynne.

And then bespake the heire of Lynne
  To John o' the Scales wife thus sayd hee,
Sayd "Dame, wilt thou not trust me one shott
  That I may sit downe in this company?"

"Now Christ's curse on my head," she said,
  "If I do trust thee one pennye,"
Then bespake a good fellowe,
  Which sate by John o' the Scales his knee,

Said "have thou here, thou heire of Lynne,
  Forty-pence I will lend thee,—
Some time a good fellow thou hast beene,
  And other forty if it need bee."

They drunken wine that was so cleere,
  And every man they made merry,
And then bespake him John o' the Scales
  Unto the Lord of Lynne said hee;

Said "how doest thou heire of Lynne,
  Since I did buy thy lands of thee?
I will sell it to thee twenty better cheepe
  Nor ever did I buy it of thee."

"I draw you to recorde, lords all:"
  With that he cast him god's penny;
Then he tooke to his bags of bread,
  And they were full of the gold so red.

He told him the gold then over the borde
   It wanted never a broad pennye;
"That gold is thine, the land is mine,
   And the heire of Lynne againe I will bee."

"Now well-a-day!" said John o' the Scales' wife,
   "Well-a-day, and woe is me!
Yesterday I was the lady of Lynne,
   And now I am but John o' the Scales' wife!"

Says "have thou here, thou good fellow,
Forty pence thou did lend me;
Forty pence thou did lend me,
And forty I will give thee,
I'll make thee keeper of my forrest,
Both of the wild deere and the tame."

But then bespake the heire of Lynne,
   These were the words and thus spake hee,
"Christ's curse light upon my crowne
   If ere my land stand in any jeopardye!"

GORDON OF BRACKLEY

Down Deeside cam Inveraye
    Whistlin' and playing,
An' called loud at Brackley gate
    Ere the day dawning—
"Come, Gordon of Brackley,
    Proud Gordon, come down,
There's a sword at your threshold
    Mair sharp than your own."

"Arise now, gay Gordon,"
    His lady 'gan cry,
"Look, here is bold Inveraye
    Driving your kye."
"How can I go, lady,
    An' win them again,
When I have but ae sword,
    And Inveraye ten?"

"Arise up, my maidens,
    Wi' roke and wi' fan,
How blest had I been
    Had I married a man!
Arise up, my maidens,
    Tak' spear and tak' sword,
Go milk the ewes, Gordon,
    An' I will be lord."

The Gordon sprung up
 Wi' his helm on his head,
Laid his hand on his sword,
 An' his thigh on his steed,
An' he stooped low, and said,
 As he kissed his young dame,
"There's a Gordon rides out
 That will never ride hame."

There rode with fierce Inverayc
 Thirty and three,
But wi' Brackley were nane
 But his brother and he;
Twa gallanter Gordons
 Did never blade draw,
But against three-and-thirty
 Wae's me! what are twa?

Wi' sword and wi' dagger
 They rushed on him rude;
The twa gallant Gordons
 Lie bathed in their blude.
Frae the springs o' the Dee
 To the mouth o' the Tay,
The Gordons mourn for him,
 And curse Inverayc.

"O were ye at Brackley?
 An' what saw ye there?
Was his young widow weeping
 An' tearing her hair?"
"I looked in at Brackley,
 I looked in, and oh!
There was mirth, there was feasting,
 But naething o' woe.

"As a rose bloomed the lady,
 An' blithe as a bride,
As a bridegroom bold Inveraye
 Smiled by her side.

Oh! she feasted him there
  As she ne'er feasted lord,
While the blood of her husband
  Was moist on his sword.

" In her chamber she kept him
  Till morning grew gray,
Thro' the dark woods of Brackley
  She shewed him the way.
'Yon wild hill,' she said,
  ' Where the sun's shining on,
Is the hill of Glentanner,—
  One kiss, and begone!'"

There's grief in the cottage,
  There's grief in the ha',
For the gude, gallant Gordon'
  That's dead an' awa',
To the bush comes the bud,
  An' the flower to the plain,
But the gude and the brave
  They come never again.

EDWARD, EDWARD.

"Why does your brand sae drop wi' blude,
   Edward, Edward?
Why does your brand sae drop wi' blude
  And why sae sad gang ye, O?"
"O I hae killed my hawk sae gude,
   Mither, mither;
O I hae killed my hawk sae gude,
  And I hae nae mair but he, O."

"Your hawk's blude was never sae red,
   Edward, Edward;
Your hawk's blude was never sae red,
  My dear son, I tell thee, O."
"O I hae killed my red-roan steed,
   Mither, mither;
O I hae killed my red-roan steed,
  That was sae fair and free, O."

"Your steed was auld, and ye've plenty mair,
   Edward, Edward;
Your steed was auld, and ye've plenty mair;
  Some ither dule ye dree, O."
"O I hae killed my father dear,
   Mither, mither;
O I hae killed my father dear,
  Alas, and wae is me, O!"

"And whatten penance will ye dree for that,
   Edward, Edward?
Whatten penance will ye dree for that?
  My dear son, now tell me, O."

"I'll set my feet in yonder boat,
    Mither, mither;
I'll set my feet in yonder boat,
    And I'll fare over the sea, O."

"And what will ye do wi' your tow'rs and
        your ha',
        Edward, Edward?
And what will ye do wi' your tow'rs and
        your ha',
    That were sae fair to see, O?"
"I'll let them stand till they doun fa',
    Mither, mither;
I'll let them stand till they doun fa',
    For here never mair maun I be, O."

"And what will ye leave to your bairns and
        your wife,
        Edward, Edward?
And what will ye leave to your bairns and
        your wife,
    When ye gang ower the sea, O?"
"The warld's room: let them beg through
        life,
        Mither, mither;
The warld's room: let them beg through life;
    For them never mair will I see, O."

"And what will ye leave to your ain mither
        dear,
        Edward, Edward?
And what will ye leave to your ain mither
        dear,
    My dear son, now tell me, O?"
"The curse of hell frae me sall ye bear,
    Mither, mither;
The curse of hell frae me sall ye bear:
    Sic counsels ye gave to me, O!"

YOUNG BENJIE

Of all the maids of fair Scotland,
    The fairest was Marjorie;
And young Benjie was her ae true love,
    And a dear true love was he.

And wow but they were lovers dear,
    And lov'd full constantlie;
But aye the mair when they fell out,
    The sairer was their plea.

And they ha'e quarrell'd on a day,
    Till Marjorie's heart grew wae;
And she said she'd chuse another luve,
    And let young Benjie gae.

And he was stout and proud-hearted,
    And thought o't bitterlie;
And he's gane by the wan moonlight,
    To meet his Marjorie.

"Oh, open, open, my true love,
    Oh, open and let me in!"
"I darena open, young Benjie,
    My three brothers are within."

"Ye lee, ye lee, ye bonnie burd,
    Sae loud's I hear ye lee;
As I came by the Louden banks,
    They bade gude e'en to me.

"But fare ye weel, my ae fause love,
   That I have lov'd sae lang!
It sets ye chuse another love,
   And let young Benjie gang."

Then Marjorie turn'd her round about,
   The tear blinding her e'e;
"I darena, darena let thee in,
   But I'll come down to thee."

Then saft she smil'd, and said to him—
   "Oh, what ill ha'e I done?"
He took her in his arms twa,
   And threw her o'er the linn.

The stream was strong, the maid was stout,
   And laith, laith to be dang;
But ere she wan the Louden banks,
   Her fair colour was wan.

Then up bespake her eldest brother—
   "Oh, see na ye what I see?"
And out then spake her second brother—
   "It is our sister Marjorie!"

Out then spake her eldest brother—
   "Oh, how shall we her ken?"
And out then spake her youngest brother—
   "There's a honey mark on her chin."

Then they've ta'en the comely corpse,
   And laid it on the ground;
Saying—"Wha has kill'd our ae sister?
   And how can he be found?

"The night it is her low lykewake,
   The morn her burial day;
And we maun watch at mirk midnight,
   And hear what she will say."

With doors ajar, and candles light,
    And torches burning clear,
The streekit corpse, till still midnight,
    They waked, but naething hear.

About the middle of the night
    The cocks began to craw;
And at the dead hour of the night,
    The corpse began to thraw.

"Oh, wha has done thee wrang, sister,
    Or dared the deadly sin?
Wha was sae stout, and fear'd nae dout,
    As throw ye o'er the linn?"

"Young Benjie was the first ae man
    I laid my love upon;
He was sae stout and proud-hearted,
    He threw me o'er the linn."

"Shall we young Benjie head, sister?
    Shall we young Benjie hang?
Or shall we pike out his twa gray een,
    And punish him ere he gang"

"Ye maunna Benjie head, brothers,
    Ye maunna Benjie hang;
But ye maun pike out his twa gray een,
    And punish him ere he gang.

"Tie a green gravat round his neck,
    And lead him out and in,
And the best ae servant about your house
    To wait young Benjie on.

"And aye at every seven years' end,
    Ye'll take him to the linn;
For that's the penance he maun dree,
    To scug his deadly sin."

AULD MAITLAND

There lived a king in southern land,
   King Edward hight his name;
Unwordily he wore the crown,
   Till fifty years were gane.

He had a sister's son o's ain,
   Was large of blood and bane;
And afterward, when he came up,
   Young Edward hight his name.

One day he came before the king,
   And kneel'd low on his knee:
"A boon, a boon, my good uncle,
   I crave to ask of thee!

"At our lang wars, in fair Scotland,
   I fain ha'e wish'd to be;
If fifteen hundred waled wight men
   You'll grant to ride with me."

"Thou shall ha'e thae, thou shall ha'e mae;
   I say it sickerlie;
And I myself, an auld gray man,
   Array'd your host shall see."

King Edward rade, King Edward ran—
   I wish him dool and pyne!
Till he had fifteen hundred men
   Assembled on the Tyne.

Ballads

And thrice as many at Berwicke
  Were all for battle bound,
[Who, marching forth with false Dunbar,
  A ready welcome found.]

They lighted on the banks of Tweed,
  And blew their coals sae het,
And fired the Merse and Teviotdale,
  All in an evening late.

As they fared up o'er Lammermoor,
  They burn'd baith up and down,
Until they came to a darksome house,
  Some call it Leader-Town.

"Wha hauds this house?" young Edward cried,
  "Or wha gi'est o'er to me?"
A gray-hair'd knight set up his head,
  And crackit right crousely:

"Of Scotland's king I haud my house;
  He pays me meat and fee;
And I will keep my gude auld house,
  While my house will keep me."

They laid their sowies to the wall,
  With mony a heavy peal;
But he threw o'er to them agen
  Baith pitch and tar barrel.

With springalds, stanes, and gads of airn,
  Amang them fast he threw;
Till mony of the Englishmen
  About the wall he slew.

Full fifteen days that braid host lay,
  Sieging Auld Maitland keen;
Syne they ha'e left him, hail and feir,
  Within his strength of stane.

Then fifteen barks, all gaily good,
   Met them upon a day,
Which they did lade with as much spoil
   As they cou'd bear away.

"England's our ain by heritage;
   And what can us withstand,
Now we ha'e conquer'd fair Scotland,
   With buckler, bow, and brand?"

Then they are on to the land of France,
   Where auld king Edward lay,
Burning baith castle, tower, and town,
   That he met in his way.

Until he came unto that town,
   Which some call Billop-Grace:
There were Auld Maitland's sons, all three,
   Learning at school, alas!

The eldest to the youngest said,
   "Oh, see ye what I see?
If all be true yon standard says,
   We're fatherless all three.

"For Scotland's conquer'd up and down;
   Landmen we'll never be!
Now, will you go, my brethren two,
   And try some jeopardy?"

Then they ha'e saddled twa black horse,
   Twa black horse and a gray;
And they are on to king Edward's host,
   Before the dawn of day.

When they arrived before the host,
   They hover'd on the lay:
"Wilt thou lend me our king's standard,
   To bear a little way?"

"Where wast thou bred? where wast thou
 born?
 Where, or in what countrie?"
"In north of England I was born;"
 (It needed him to lee.)

"A knight me gat, a ladye bore,
 I am a squire of high renown;
I well may bear't to any king
 That ever yet wore crown."

"He ne'er came of an Englishman,
 Had sic an e'e or bree;
But thou art the likest Auld Maitland,
 That ever I did see.

"But sic a gloom on ae browhead,
 Grant I ne'er see again!
For mony of our men he slew,
 And mony put to pain."

When Maitland heard his father's name,
 An angry man was he;
Then, lifting up a gilt dagger,
 Hung low down by his knee,

He stabb'd the knight the standard bore,
 He stabb'd him cruellie;
Then caught the standard by the neuk,
 And fast away rode he.

"Now, is't na time, brothers," he cried,
 "Now, is't na time to flee?"
"Ay, by my sooth!" they baith replied,
 "We'll bear you companye."

The youngest turn'd him in a path,
 And drew a burnish'd brand,
And fifteen of the foremost slew,
 Till back the lave did stand.

He spurr'd the gray into the path,
  Till baith his sides they bled :
" Gray ! thou maun carry me away,
  Or my life lies in wad ! "

The captain lookit o'er the wall,
  About the break of day ;
There he beheld the three Scots lads
  Pursued along the way.

" Pull up portcullize ! down draw-brig !
  My nephews are at hand ;
And they shall lodge with me to-night,
  In spite of all England."

Whene'er they came within the yate,
  They thrust their horse them frae,
And took three lang spears in their hands,
  Saying—" Here shall come nae me ! "

And they shot out, and they shot in,
  Till it was fairly day ;
When mony of the Englishmen
  About the draw-brig lay.

Then they ha'e yoked the carts and wains,
  To ca' their dead away,
And shot auld dykes abune the lave,
  In gutters where they lay.

The king, at his pavilion door,
  Was heard aloud to say :
" Last night, three of the lads of France
  My standard stole away.

" With a fause tale, disguised they came,
  And with a fauser trayne ;
And to regain my gaye standard,
  These men where all down slayne."

"It ill befits," the youngest said,
  "A crownèd king to lee;
But, or that I taste meat and drink,
  Reprovèd shall he be."

He went before king Edward straight,
  And kneel'd low on his knee:
"I wou'd ha'e leave, my lord," he said,
  "To speak a word with thee."

The king he turn'd him round about,
  And wistna what to say:
Quo' he, "Man, thou 's ha'e leave to speak,
  Though thou should speak all day."

"Ye said that three young lads of France
  Your standard stole away,
With a fause tale and fauser trayne,
  And mony men did slay;

"But we are nane the lads of France,
  Nor e'er pretend to be:
We are three lads of fair Scotland,—
  Auld Maitland's sons are we.

"Nor is there men in all your host
  Daur fight us three to three."
"Now, by my sooth," young Edward said,
  "Weel fitted ye shall be!

"Piercy shall with the eldest fight,
  And Ethert Lunn with thee;
William of Lancaster the third,
  And bring your fourth to me!

"Remember, Piercy, aft the Scot
  Has cower'd beneath thy hand;
For every drap of Maitland blood,
  I'll gi'e a rig of land."

He clanked Piercy o'er the head
   A deep wound and a sair,
Till the best blood of his body
   Came running down his hair.

" Now, I've slayne ane ; slay ye the twa ;
   And that's gude companye ;
And if the twa shou'd slay ye baith,
   Ye'se get nae help frae me."

But Ethert Lunn, a baited bear,
   Had many battles seen ;
He set the youngest wonder sair,
   Till the eldest he grew keen.

" I am nae king, nor nae sic thing :
   My word it shanna stand !
For Ethert shall a buffet bide,
   Come he beneath my brand."

He clankit Ethert o'er the head
   A deep wound and a sair,
Till the best blood in his body
   Came running o'er his hair.

" Now, I've slayne twa ; slay ye the ane ;
   Isna that gude companye ?
And though the ane shou'd slay ye baith,
   Ye'se get nae help of me."

The twa-some they ha'e slayne the ane,
   They maul'd him cruellie ;
Then hung him over the draw-brig,
   That all the host might see.

They rade their horse, they ran their horse,
   Then hover'd on the lee :
" We be three lads of fair Scotland,
   That fain wou'd fighting see."

This boasting when young Edward heard;
 An angry man was he:
"I'll take yon lad, I'll bind yon lad,
 And bring him bound to thee!"

"Now, God forbid," king Edward said,
 "That ever thou shou'd try!
Three worthy leaders we ha'e lost,
 And thou the forth wou'd lie.

"If thou shou'dst hang on yon draw-brig,
 Blythe wou'd I never be."
But, with the poll-axe in his hand,
 Upon the brig sprang he.

The first stroke that young Edward ga'e,
 He struck with might and main;
He clove the Maitland's helmet stout,
 And bit right nigh the brain.

When Maitland saw his ain blood fall,
 An angry man was he;
He let his weapon frae him fall,
 And at his throat did flee.

And thrice about he did him swing,
 Till on the ground he light,
Where he has halden young Edward,
 Tho' he was great in might.

"Now let him up," king Edward cried,
 "And let him come to me;
And for the deed that thou hast done,
 Thou shalt ha'e earldomes three!"

"It's ne'er be said in France, nor e'er
 In Scotland, when I'm hame,
That Edward once lay under me,
 And e'er gat up again!"

He pierced him through and through the heart,
  He maul'd him cruellie;
Then hung him o'er the draw-brig,
  Beside the other three.

"Now take frae me that feather-bed,
  Make me a bed of strae!
I wish I hadna lived this day,
  To make my heart sae wae.

"If I were ance at London Tow'r,
  Where I was wont to be,
I never mair shou'd gang frae hame,
  Till borne on a bier-tree."

THE BROOMFIELD HILL

THERE was a knight and lady bright
   Set trysts amo the broom,
The one to come at morning eav,
   The other at afternoon.

" I'll wager a wager wi' you," he said,
   " An hundred marks and ten,
That ye shall not go to Broomfield Hills,
   Return a maiden again."

" I'll wager a wager wi' you," she said,
   " A hundred pounds and ten,
That I will gang to Broomfield Hills,
   A maiden return again."

The lady stands in her bower door,
   And thus she made her mane :
" Oh, shall I gang to Broomfield Hills,
   Or shall I stay at hame?

" If I do gang to Broomfield Hills
   A maid I'll not return ;
But if I stay from Broomfield Hills,
   I'll be a maid mis-sworn."

Then out it speaks an auld witch wife,
   Sat in the bower aboon :
" O ye shall gang to Broomfield Hills,
   Ye shall not stay at hame.

"But when ye gang to Broomfield Hills,
   Walk nine times round and round;
Down below a bonny burn bank,
   Ye'll find your love sleeping sound.

"Ye'll pu the bloom frae off the broom,
   Strew't at his head and feet,
And aye the thicker that ye do strew,
   The sounder he will sleep.

"The broach that is on your napkin,
   Put it on his breast bane,
To let him know, when he does wake,
   That's true love's come and gane.

"The rings that are on your fingers,
   Lay them down on a stane,
To let him know, when he does wake,
   That's true love's come and gane.

"And when he hae your work all done,
   Ye'll gang to a bush o' broom,
And then you'll hear what he will say,
   When he sees ye are gane."

When she came to Broomfield Hills,
   She walked it nine times round,
And down below yon burn bank,
   She found him sleeping sound.

She pu'd the bloom frae off the broom,
   Strew'd it at 's head and feet,
And aye the thicker that she strewd,
   The sounder he did sleep.

The broach that was on her napkin,
   She put it on his breast-bane,
To let him know, when he did wake,
   His love was come and gane.

The rings that were on her fingers,
    She laid upon a stane,
To let him know, when he did wake,
    His love was come and gane.

Now when she had her work all dune,
    She went to a bush o' broom,
That she might hear what he did say,
    When he saw that she was gane.

"O where were ye my guid grey hound,
    That I paid for sae dear,
Ye didna waken me frae my sleep
    When my true love was sae near?"

"I scraped wi' my foot, master,
    Till a' my collars rang,
But still the mair that I did scrape,
    Waken woud ye nane."

"Where were ye, my bony brown steed,
    That I paid for sae dear,
That ye woudna waken me out o' my sleep
    When my love was sae near?"

"I patted wi my foot, master,
    Till a' my bridles rang,
But the mair that I did patt,
    Waken woud ye nane."

"O where were ye, my gay goss-hawk
    That I paid for sae dear,
That ye woudna waken me out o' my sleep
    When ye saw my love near?"

"I flapped wi my wings, master,
    Till a' my bells they rang,
But still, the mair that I did flap,
    Waken woud ye nane."

"O where were ye, my merry young men,
　　That I pay meat and fee,
That ye woudna waken me out o' my sleep
　　When my love ye did see?"

"Ye'll sleep mair on the night, master,
　　And wake mair on the day;
Gae sooner down to Broomfield Hills
　　When ye've sic pranks to play.

"If I had seen any armèd men
　　Come riding over the hill—
But I saw but a fair lady
　　Come quietly you until."

"O wae mat worth yow, my young men,
　　That I pay meat and fee,
That ye woudna waken me frae sleep
　　When ye my love did see?

"O had I waked when she was nigh,
　　And o her got my will,
I shoudna cared upon the morn
　　The sma birds o her were fill."

When she went out, right bitter she wept,
　　But singing came she hame;
Says, "I hae been at Broomfield Hills,
　　And maid returned again."

WILLIE'S LADYE

WILLIE has ta'en him o'er the faem,
He 's wooed a wife, and brought her hame ;
He 's wooed her for her yellow hair,
But his mother wrought her meikle care ;

And meikle dolour gar'd her dree,
For lighter she can never be ;
But in her bow'r she sits with pain,
And Willie mourns o'er her in vain.

And to his mother he has gane,
That vile rank witch, of vilest kind !
He says—" My lady has a cup,
With gowd and silver set about ;
This gudely gift shall be your ain,
And let her be lighter of her bairn."

"Of her bairn she 's never be lighter,
Nor in her bow'r to shine the brighter
But she shall die, and turn to clay,
And you shall wed another may."

" Another may I'll never wed,
Another may I'll never bring hame."
But, sighing, said that weary wight—
" I wish my life were at an end."

" Yet gae ye to your mother again,
That vile rank witch, of vilest kind
And say, your ladye has a steed,
The like of him 's no in the land of Leed.

"For he is silver shod before,
And he is gowden shod behind;
At every tuft of that horse mane
There's a golden chess, and a bell to ring.
This gudely gift shall be her ain,
And let me be lighter of my bairn."

"Of her young bairn she 's ne'er be lighter,
Nor in her bow'r to shine the brighter;
But she shall die, and turn to clay,
And ye shall wed another may."

"Another may I'll never wed,
Another may I'll never bring hame."
But, sighing, said that weary wight—
"I wish my life were at an end!"

"Yet gae ye to your mother again,
That vile rank witch, of rankest kind!
And say, your ladye has a girdle,
It 's all red gowd to the middle;

"And aye, at ilka siller hem,
Hang fifty siller bells and ten;
This gudely gift shall be her ain,
And let me be lighter of my bairn."

"Of her young bairn she 's ne'er be lighter,
Nor in your bow'r to shine the brighter;
For she shall die, and turn to clay,
And thou shall wed another may."

"Another may I'll never wed,
Another may I'll never bring hame."
But, sighing, said that weary wight—
"I wish my days were at an end!"

Then out and spak the Billy Blind,
He spak aye in good time [his mind]:—
"Yet gae ye to the market place,
And there do buy a loaf of wace;
Do shape it bairn and bairnly like,
And in it two glassen een you'll put.

"Oh, wha has loosed the nine witch-knots
That were amang that ladye's locks?
And wha 's ta'en out the kames of care,
That were amang that ladye's hair?

"And wha has ta'en down that bush of woodbine
That hung between her bow'r and mine?
And wha has kill'd the master kid
That ran beneath that ladye's bed?
And wha has loosed her left foot shee,
And let that ladye lighter be?"

Syne, Willie 's loosed the nine witch-knots
That were amang that ladye's locks;
And Willie 's ta'en out the kames of care
That were into that ladye's hair;
And he 's ta'en down the bush of woodbine
Hung atween her bow'r and the witch carline'.

And he has killed the master kid
That ran beneath that ladye's bed;
And he has loosed her left foot shee,
And latten that ladye lighter be;
And now he has gotten a bonnie son,
And meikle grace be him upon.

ROBIN HOOD AND THE MONK

IN somer when the shawes be sheyne,
  And leves be large and longe,
Hit is full mery in feyre foreste
  To here the foulys song.

To se the dere draw to the dale,
  And leve the hilles hee,
And shadow hem in the leves grene,
  Vndur the grene-wode tre.

Hit befell on Whitsontide,
  Erly in a may mornyng,
The son vp fayre can shyne,
  And the briddis mery can syng.

"This is a mery mornyng," seid Litul
    Johne,
  "Be hym that dyed on tre;
A more mery man than I am one
  Lyves not in Cristianté."

"Pluk vp thi hert, my dere mayster,"
    Litulle Johne can sey,
"And thynk hit is a fulle fayre tyme
  In a mornynge of may."

"Ze on thynge greves me," seid Robyne,
  "And does my hert mych woo,
That I may not so solem day
  To mas nor matyns goo.

"Hit is a fourtnet and more," seyd hee,
"Syn I my Sauyour see;
To day will I to Notyngham," seid Robyn,
"With the myght of mylde Mary."

Then spake Moche the mylner sune,
Euer more wel hym betyde,
"Take xii of thi wyght zemen
Well weppynd be thei side.
Such on wolde thi selfe slon
That xii dar not abyde."

"Off alle my mery men," seid Robyne,
"Be my feithe I wil non haue;
But Litulle Johne shall beyre my bow
Til that me list to drawe."

. . . . . .
. . . . .

"Thou shalle beyre thin own," seid Litulle Jon,
"Maister, and I wil beyre myne,
And we wille shete a peny," seid Litulle Jon,
"Vnder the grene wode lyne."

"I wil not shete a peny," seyde Robyn Hode,
"In feith, Litulle Johne, with thee,
But euer for on as thou shetes," seid Robyn,
"In feith I holde the thre."

Thus shet thei forthe, these zemen too,
Bothe at buske and brome,
Til Litulle Johne wan of his maister
V s. to hose and shone.

A ferly strife fel them betwene,
  As they went bi the way;
Litull Johne seid he had won v shyllyngs,
  And Robyn Hode seid schortly nay.

With that Robyn Hode lyed Litul Jone,
  And smote him with his honde;
Litul John waxed wroth therwith,
  And pulled out his bright bronde.

"Were thou not my maister," seid Litulle
    Johne,
  "Thou shuldis by hit ful sore;
Get the a man where thou wilt, Robyn,
  For thou getes me no more."

Then Robyn goes to Notyngham,
  Hymselfe mornynge allone,
And Litulle Johne to mery Scherewode,
  The pathes he knowe alkone.

Whan Robyn came to Notyngham,
  Sertenly withoutene layne,
He prayed to God and myld Mary
  To brynge hym out saue agayne.

He gos into seynt Mary chirche,
  And knelyd downe before the rode;
Alle that euer were the churche within
  Beheld wel Robyne Hode.

Beside hym stode a gret-hedid munke,
  I pray to God woo he be;
Full sone he knew gode Robyn
  As sone as he hym se.

Out at the durre he ran
  Ful sone and anon;
Alle the zatis of Notyngham
  He made to be sparred euerychone.

"Rise vp," he seid, "thou prowde schereff,
　Buske the and make the bowne;
I haue spyed the kynges felone,
　For sothe he is in this towne.

"I haue spyed the false felone,
　As he stondes at his masse;
Hit is longe of the," seide the munke,
　"And euer he fro vs passe.

"This traytur[s] name is Robyn Hode;
　Vnder the grene wode lynde,
He robbyt me onys of a C pound,
　Hit shalle neuer out of my mynde."

Vp then rose this prowd schereff,
　And zade towarde hym zare;
Many was the modur son
　To the kyrk with him can fare.

In at the durres thei throly thrast
　With staves ful gode ilkone,
"Alas, alas," seid Robin Hode,
　"Now mysse I Litulle Johne."

But Robyne toke out a too-hond sworde
　That hangit down be his kne;
Ther as the schereff and his men stode thyckust,
　Thidurward wold he.

Thryes thorow at them he ran,
　Then for sothe as I yow say,
And woundyt many a modur sone,
　And xii he slew that day.

Hys sworde vpon the schireff hed
  Sertanly he brake in too;
"The smyth that the made," seid Robyn,
  "I pray God wyrke him woo.

"For now am I weppynlesse," seid Robyne,
  "Alasse, agayn my wylle;
But if I may fle these traytors fro,
  I wot thei wil me kylle."

Robyns men to the churche ran
  Throout hem euerilkon;
Sum fel in swonyng as thei were dede,
  And lay still as any stone.

    .   .   .   .   .   .

Non of theym were in her mynde
  But only Litulle Jon.

"Let be your dule," seid Litulle Jon,
  "For his luf that dyed on tre;
Ze that shulde be duzty men,
  Hit is gret shame to se.

"Oure maister has bene hard bystode,
  And zet scapyd away;
Pluk up your hertes and leve this mone,
  And herkyn what I shal say.

"He has seruyd our lady many a day,
  And zet wil securly;
Therefore I trust in her specialy
  No wycked deth shal he dye.

"Therfor be glad," seid Litul Johne,
  "And let this mournyng be,
And I shall be the munkes gyde,
  With the myght of mylde Mary.

"And I mete hym," seid Litull Johne,
 "We will go but we too
. . . . . .
 . . . . .

"Loke that ze kepe wel our tristil tre
 Vnder the levys smale,
And spare non of this venyson
 That gose in thys vale."

Forthe thei went these zemen too,
 Litul Johne and Moche onfere,
And lokid on Moche emys hows
 The hyeway lay fulle nere.

Litul John stode at a window in the
 mornynge,
 And lokid forth at a stage;
He was war wher the munke came ridynge,
 And with him a litul page.

"Be my feith," said Litul Johne to Moche,
 "I can the tel tithyngus gode;
I se wher the munk comys rydyng,
 I know hym be his wyde hode."

Thei went into the way these zemen bothe
 As curtes men and hende,
Thei spyrred tithyngus at the munke,
 As thei hade bene his frende.

"Fro whens come ze," seid Litul Johne,
 "Tel vs tithyngus, I yow pray,
Off a false owtlay [called Robyn Hode],
 Was takyn zisturday.

"He robbyt me and my felowes bothe
 Of xx marke in serten;
If that false owtlay be takyn,
 For sothe we wolde be fayne."

"So did he me," seid the munke,
　"Of a C pound and more;
I layde furst hande hym apon,
　Ze may thonke me therefore."

"I pray God thanke yow," seid Litulle Johne,
　"And we wil when we may;
We wil go with yow, with your leve,
　And brynge yow on your way.

"For Robyn Hode hase many a wilde felow,
　I telle yow in certen;
If thei wist ze rode this way,
　In feith ze shulde be slayn."

As thei went talkyng be the way,
　The munke and Litulle Johne,
Johne toke the munkes horse be the hede
　Ful sone and anone.

Johne toke the munkes horse be the hed,
　For sothe as I yow say,
So did Muche the litulle page,
　For he shulde not stirre away.

Be the golett of the hode
　Johne pulled the munke downe;
Johne was nothynge of hym agast,
　He lete hym falle on his crowne.

Litulle Johne was sore agrevyd,
　And drew out his swerde in hye;
The munke saw he shulde be ded,
　Lowd mercy can he crye.

"He was my maister," said Litulle Johne,
 "That thou hasc browzt in bale;
Shalle thou neuer cum at our kynge
 For to telle hym tale."

John smote of the munkes hed,
 No longer wolde he dwelle;
So did Moche the litulle page,
 For ferd lest he wold tell.

Ther thei beryed hem both
 In nouther mosse nor lynge,
And Litulle Johne and Muche infere
 Bare the letturs to oure kyng.

. . . . .

He kneled down vpon his kne,
 "God zow saue, my lege lorde,
Jesus yow saue and se.

"God yow saue, my lege kyng,"
 To speke Johne was fulle bolde;
He gaf hym the letturs in his hond,
 The kyng did hit vnfold.

The kyng red the letturs anon,
 And seid, "so mot I the,
Ther was neuer zoman in mery Inglond
 I longut so sore to see.

"Wher is the munke that these shuld
  haue browzt?"
 Oure kynge gan say;
"Be my trouthe," seid Litull Jone,
 "He dyed aftur the way."

The kyng gaf Moche and Litul Jon
 xx pound in sertan,
And made theim zemen of the crowne,
 And bade theim go agayn.

He gaf Johne the seel in hand,
    The scheref for to bere,
To brynge Robyn hym to,
    And no man do hym dere.

Johne toke his leve at oure kyng,
    The sothe as I yow say;
The next way to Notyngham
    To take he zede the way.

When Johne came to Notynghani
    The zatis were sparred ychone;
Johne callid vp the porter,
    He answerid sone anon.

"What is the cause," seid Litul John,
    "Thou sparris the zates so fast?"
"Because of Robyn Hode," seid [the] porter,
    "In depe prison is cast.

"Johne, and Moche, and Wylle Scathlok,
    For sothe as I yow say,
Thir slew oure men vpon oure wallis,
    And sawtene vs euery day."

Litulle Johne spyrred aftur the schereff,
    And sone he hym fonde;
He oppyned the kyngus privè seelle,
    And gaf hym in his honde.

When the schereft saw the kyngus seelle,
    He did of his hode anon;
"Wher is the munke that bare the letturs?"
    He seid to Litulle Johne.

"He is so fayn of hym," seid Litulle Johne,
 "For sothe as I yow sey,
He has made hym abot of Westmynster,
 A lorde of that abbay."

The scheref made John gode chere,
 And gaf hym wine of the best;
At nyzt thei went to her bedde,
 And euery man to his rest.

When the scheref was on-slepe
 Dronken of wine and ale,
Litul Johne and Moche for sothe
 Toke the way vnto the jale.

Litul Johne callid vp the jayler,
 And bade him rysc anon;
He seid Robyn Hode had brokyn preson,
 And out of hit was gon.

The portere rose anon sertan,
 As sone as he herd John calle;
Litul Johne was redy with a swerd,
 And bare hym to the walle.

"Now will I be porter," seid Litul Johne,
 "And take the keyes in honde;"
He toke the way to Robyn Hode,
 And sone he hym vnbonde.

He gaf hym a gode swerd in his hond,
 His hed with for to kepe,
And ther as the walle was lowyst
 Anon down can thei lepe.

Be that the cok began to crow,
 The day began to sprynge,
The scheref fond the jaylier ded,
 The comyn belle made he rynge.

He made a crye thoroowt al the tow[n],
  Whedur he be zoman or knave,
That cowthe brynge hym Robyn Hode,
  His warisone he shuld haue.

"For I dar neuer," said the scheref,
  "Cum before oure kynge,
For if I do, I wot serten,
  For sothe he wil me henge."

The scheref made to seke Notyngham,
  Bothe be strete and stye,
And Robyn was in mery Scherwode
  As lizt as lef on lynde.

Then bespake gode Litulle Johne,
  To Robyn Hode can he say,
"I haue done the a gode turne for an euylle,
  Quyte me whan thou may.

"I haue done the a gode turne," said Litulle Johne,
  "For sothe as I you saie;
I haue brouzt the vnder grene wode lyne;
  Fare wel, and haue gode day."

"Nay, be my trouthe," seid Robyn Hode,
  "So shalle hit neuer be;
I make the maister," seid Robyn Hode,
  "Off alle my men and me."

"Nay, be my trouthe," seid Litulle Johne,
  "So shall hit neuer be,
But lat me be a felow," seid Litulle Johne,
  "Non odur kepe I'll be."

Thus Johne gate Robyn Hode out of
    prisone,
  Sertan withoutyn layne;
When his men saw hym hol and sounde,
  For sothe they were ful fayne.

They filled in wyne, and made him glad,
  Vnder the levys smale,
And zete pastes of venysone,
  That gode was with ale.

Than worde came to oure kynge,
  How Robyn Hode was gone,
And how the scheref of Notyngham
  Durst neuer loke hyme vpone.

Then bespake oure cumly kynge,
  In an angur hye,
"Litulle Johne hase begyled the schereff,
  In faith so hase he me.

"Litulle Johne has begyled vs bothe,
  And that fulle wel I se,
Or ellis the schereff of Notyngham
  Hye hongut shuld he be.

"I made hem zemen of the crowne,
  And gaf hem fee with my hond,
I gaf hem grithe," seid oure kyng,
  "Thorowout alle mery Inglond.

"I gaf hem grithe," then seide oure kyng,
  "I say, so mot I the,
For sothe soche a zeman as he is on
  In alle Ingland ar not thre.

"He is trew to his maister," seide oure
    kynge,
  "I say, be swete seynt Johne;

He louys bettur Robyn Hode,
    Then he dose vs ychone.

"Robyne Hode is euer bond to him,
    Bothe in strete and stalle;
Speke no more of this matter," seid oure
      kynge,
    "But John has begyled vs alle."

Thus endys the talkyng of the munke
    And Robyne Hode i-wysse;
God, that is euer a crowned kyng,
    Bryng vs alle to his blisse.

ROBIN HOOD AND THE POTTER

In schomer, when the leves spryng,
    The bloschems on every bowe,
So merey doyt the berdys syng
    Yn wodys merey now.

Herkens, god yemen,
    Comley, corteysse, and god,
On of the best that yever bar bou,
    Hes name was Roben Hode.

Roben Hood was the yemans name,
    That was boyt corteys and fre;
For the loffe of owr ladey,
    All wemen werschep he.

Bot as the god yemen stod on a day,
    Among hes mery manèy,
He was war of a prowd potter,
    Cam dryfyng owyr the ley.

"Yonder comet a prod potter," seyde Roben,
    "That long hayt hantyd this wey;
He was never so corteys a man
    On peney of pawage to pay."

"Y met hem bot at Wentbreg," seyde Lytyll John,
    "And therfor yeffell mot he the,
Seche thre strokes he me gafe,
    Yet they cleffe by my seydys.

"Y ley forty shillings," seyde Lytyll John,
  "To pay het thes same day,
Ther ys nat a man among hus all
  A wed schall make hem ley."

"Her ys forty shillings," seyde Roben,
  "Mor, and thow dar say,
That y schall make that prowde potter,
  A wed to me schall he ley."

Ther thes money they leyde,
  They toke het a yeman to kepe;
Roben befor the potter he breyde,
  And bad hem stond stell.

Handys apon hes horse he leyde,
  And bad the potter stonde foll stell;
The potter schorteley to hem seyde,
  "Felow, what ys they well?"

"All thes thre yer, and mor, potter," he seyde,
  "Thow hast hantyd thes wey,
Yet wer tow never so cortys a man
  One peney of pauage to pay."

"What ys they name," seyde the potter,
  "For pauage thow ask of me?"
"Roben Hod ys mey name,
  A wed schall thow leffe me."

"Wed well y non leffe," seyde the potter,
  "Nor pavag well y non pay;
Away they honde fro mey horse,
  Y well the tene eyls, be me fay."

The potter to hes cart he went,
  He was not to seke;
A god to-hande staffe therowt he hent,
  Befor Roben he lepe.

Roben howt with a swerd bent,
   A bokeler en hes honde [therto];
The potter to Roben he went,
   And seyde, "Felow, let mey horse go."

Togeder then went thes two yemen,
   Het was a god seyt to se;
Therof low Robyn hes men,
   Ther they stod onder a tre.

Leytell John to hes felowhes seyde,
   "Yend potter welle steffeley stonde:"
The potter, with an acward stroke,
   Smot the bokeler owt of hes honde;

And ar Roben meyt get hem agen
   Hes bokeler at hes fette,
The potter yn the neke hem toke,
   To the gronde sone he yede.

That saw Roben hes men,
   As they stode ender a bow;
"Let us helpe owr master," seyed Lytell John,
   "Yonder potter els well hem sclo."

Thes yemen went with a breyde,
   To ther master they cam.
Leytell John to hes master seyde,
   "He haet the wager won?"

"Schall y haff yowr forty shillings,"
   seyde Lytel John,
   "Or ye, master, schall haffe myne?"
'Yeff they wer a hundred," seyde Roben,
   "Y feythe, they ben all theyne."

"Het ys fol leytell cortesey," seyde the
    potter,
  "As y haffe harde weyse men saye,
Yeff a por yeman com drywyng ower the
    wey,
  To let hem of hes gorney."

"Be mey trowet, thow seys soyt," seyde
    Roben,
  "Thow seys god yemenrey;
And thow dreyffe forthe yevery day,
  Thow schalt never be let for me.

"Y well prey the, god potter,
  A felischepe well thow haffe?
Geffe me they clothyng, and thow schalt
    hafe myne;
  Y well go to Notynggam."

"Y grant therto," seyde the potter,
  "Thow schalt feynde me a felow gode;
But thow can sell mey pottes well,
  Come ayen as thow yode."

"Nay, be mey trowt," seyde Roben,
  "And then y bescro mey hede
Yeffe y bryng eney pottes ayen,
  And eney weyffe well hem chepe."

Than spake Leytell John,
  And all hes felowhes heynd,
"Master, be well war of the screffe of
    Notynggam,
  For he ys leytell howr frende."

"Heyt war howte," seyde Roben,
  "Felowhes, let me alone;
Thorow the helpe of howr ladey,
  To Notynggam well y gon."

Robyn went to Notynggam,
    Thes pottes for to sell;
The potter abode with Robens men,
    Ther he fered not eylle.

Tho Roben droffe on hes wey,
    So merey ower the londe:
Heres mor and affter ys to saye,
    The best ys beheynde.

[THE SECOND FIT.]

WHEN Roben cam to Netynggam,
    The soyt yef y scholde saye,
He set op hes horse anon,
    And gaffe hem hotys and haye.

Yn the medys of the towne,
    Ther he schowed hes war;
"Pottys! pottys!" he gan crey foll sone,
    "Haffe hansell for the mar."

Foll effen agenest the screffeys gate
    Schowed he hes chaffar;
Weyffes and wedowes abowt hem drow,
    And chepyd fast of hes war.

Yet, "Pottys, gret chepe!" creyed Robyn,
    "Y loffe yeffell thes to stonde;"
And all that saw hem sell,
    Seyde he had be no potter long.

The pottys that wer werthe pens feyffe,
    He sold tham for pens thre;
Preveley seyde man and weyffe,
    "Ywnder potter schall never the."

Thos Roben solde foll fast,
   Tell he had pottys bot feyffe;
Op he hem toke of his car,
   And sende hem to the screffeys weyffe.

Therof sche was foll fayne,
   "Gramarsey, sir," than seyde sche;
"When ye com to thes contre ayen,
   Y schall bey of they pottys, so mot y the."

"Ye schall haffe of the best," seyde Roben,
   And swar be the treneytè;
Foll corteysley she gan hem call,
   "Com deyne with the screfe and me."

"Godamarsey," seyde Roben,
   "Yowr bedyng schalle be doyn;"
A mayden yn the pottys gan ber,
   Roben and the screffe weyffe folowed anon.

Whan Roben ynto the hall cam,
   The screffe sone he met;
The potter cowed of corteysey,
   And sone the screffe he gret.

"Loketh what thes potter hayt geffe yow and me;
   Feyffe pottys smalle and grete!"
"He ys fol wellcom," seyd the screffe,
   "Let os was, and go to mete."

As they sat at her methe,
   With a nobell cher,
Two of the screffes men gan speke
   Off a gret wagèr,

Was made the thother daye,
   Off a schotyng was god and feyne,
Off forty shillings, the soyt to saye,
   Who scholde thes wager wen.

Styll than sat thes prowde potter,
   'Thos than thowt he;
"As y am a trow Cerstyn man,
   Thes schotyng well y se."

Whan they had fared of the best,
   With bred and ale and weyne,
To the bottys they made them prest,
   With bowes and boltys full feyne.

The screffes men schot foll fast,
   As archares that weren godde;
Ther cam non ner ney the marke
   Bey halfe a god archares bowe.

Stell then stod the prowde potter,
   Thos than seyde he;
"And y had a bow, be the rode,
   On schot scholde yow se."

"Thow schall haffe a bow," seyde the screffe,
   "The best that thow well cheys of thre;
Thou semyst a stalward and a stronge,
   Asay schall thow be."

The screffe commandyd a yeman that stod hem bey
   Affter bowhes to wende;
The best bow that the yeman browthe
   Roben set on a stryng.

"Now schall y wet and thow be god,
   And polle het op to they ner;"
"So god me helpe," seyde the prowde
    potter,
   "Thys ys bot rygzt weke ger."

To a quequer Roben went,
   A god bolt owthe he toke;
So ney on to the marke he went,
   He fayled not a fothe.

All they schot abowthe agen,
   The screffes men and he;
Off the marke he welde not fayle,
   He cleffed the preke on thre.

The screffes men thowt gret schame,
   The potter the mastry wan;
The screffe lowe and made god game,
   And seyde, "Potter, thow art a man;
Thow art worthey to ber a bowe,
   Yn what plas that thow gang."

"Yn mey cart y haffe a bowe,
   Forsoyt," he seyde, "and that a godde;
Yn mey cart ys the bow
   That I had of Robyn Hode."

"Knowest thow Robyn Hode?" seyde
    the screffe,
   "Potter, y prey the tell thou me;"
"A hundred torne y haffe schot with hem,
   Under hes tortyll tree."

"Y had lever nar a hundred ponde,"
    seyde the screffe,
   And swar be the trenitè,
["Y had lever nar a hundred ponde," he
    seyde,]
   "That the fals owtelawe stod be me.

"And ye well do afftyr mey red," seyde
 the potter,
 "And boldeley go with me,
And to morow, or we het bred,
 Roben Hode wel we se."

"Y well queyt the," kod the screffe,
 And swer be god of meythe ;
Schetyng thay left, and hom they went,
 Her scoper was redey deythe.

Upon the morow, when het was day,
 He boskyd hem forthe to ryde ;
The potter hes carte forthe gan ray,
 And wolde not [be] leffe beheynde.

He toke leffe of the screffys wyffe,
 And thankyd her of all thyng :
"Dam, for mey loffe, and ye well thys
 wer,
 Y geffe yow her a golde ryng."

"Gramarsey," seyde the weyffe,
 "Sir, god eylde het the ;"
The screffes hart was never so leythe,
 The feyr forest to se.

And when he cam ynto the foreyst,
 Yonder the leffes grene,
Berdys ther sange on bowhes prest,
 Het was gret joy to sene.

"Her het ys mercy to be," seyde Roben,
 "For a man that had hawt to spende ;
Be mey horne we schall awet
 Yeff Roben Hode be ner hande."

217

Roben set hes horne to hes mowthe,
   And blow a blast that was full god,
That herde hes men that ther stode,
   Fer downe yn the wodde;
"I her mey master," seyde Leytell John;
   They ran as thay wer wode.

Whan thay to thar master cam,
   Leytell John wold not spar;
"Master, how haffe yow far yn Notyng-
    gam?
   How haffe yow solde yowr war?"

"Ye, be mey trowthe, Leytyll John,
   Loke thow take no car;
Y haffe browt the screffe of Notynggam,
   For all howr chaffar."

"He ys foll wellcom," seyde Lytyll John,
   "Thes tydyng ys foll godde;"
The screffe had lever nar a hundred ponde
   [He had never sene Roben Hode.]

"Had I west that beforen,
   At Notynggam when we wer,
Thow scholde not com yn feyr forest
   Of all thes thowsande eyr."

"That wot y well," seyde Roben,
   "Y thanke god that ye be her;
Therfor schall ye leffe yowr horse with hos,
   And all your hother ger."

"That fend I godys forbode," kod the
    screffe,
   "So to lese mey godde;"
"Hether ye cam on horse foll hey,
   And hom schall ye go on fote;

And gret well they weyffe at home,
　　The woman ys foll godde.

"Y schall her sende a wheyt palffrey,
　　Het hambellet as the weynde;
Ner for the loffe of yowr weyffe,
　　Off mor sorow scholde yow seyng."

Thes parted Robyn Hode and the screffe,
　　To Notynggam he toke the waye;
Hes weyffe feyr welcomed hem hom,
　　And to hem gan sche saye:

"Seyr, how haffe yow fared yn grene foreyst?
　　Haffe ye browt Roben hom?"
"Dam, the deyell spede him, bothe bodey and bon,
　　Y haffe hade a foll grete skorne.

"Of all the god that y haffe lade to grene wod,
　　He hayt take het fro me,
All bot this feyr palffrey,
　　That he hayt sende to the."

With that sche toke op a lowde lawhyng,
　　And swhar be hem that deyed on tre,
"Now haffe yow payed for all the pottys
　　That Roben gaffe to me.

"Now ye be com hom to Notynggam,
　　Ye schall haffe god ynowe;"
Now speke we of Roben Hode,
　　And of the pottyr onder the grene bowhe.

"Potter, what was they pottys worthe
　　To Notynggam that y ledde with me?"

"They wer worth two nobellys," seyd he,
  "So mot y treyffe or the;
So cowde y had for tham,
  And y had ther be."

"Thow schalt hafe ten ponde," seyde Roben,
  "Of money feyr and fre;
And yever whan thou comest to grene wod,
  Wellcom, potter to me."

Thes partyd Robyn, the screffe, and the potter,
  Ondernethe the grene-wod tre;
God haffe mersey on Robyn Hodys solle,
  And saffe all god yemanrey!

ROBIN HOOD AND THE BUTCHER

Come, all you brave gallants, and listen awhile,
    With hey down, down, an a down,
That are in the bowers within;
For of Robin Hood, that archer good,
  A song I intend for to sing.

Upon a time it chancèd so,
  Bold Robin in forrest did 'spy
A jolly butcher, with a bonny fine mare,
  With his flesh to the market did hye.

"Good morrow, good fellow," said jolly Robin,
  "What food hast [thou]? tell unto me;
Thy trade to me tell, and where thou dost dwell,
  For I like well thy company."

The butcher he answer'd jolly Robin,
  "No matter where I dwell;
For a butcher I am, and to Nottingham
  I am going, my flesh to sell."

"What's [the] price of thy flesh?" said jolly Robin,
  "Come, tell it soon unto me;
And the price of thy mare, be she never so dear,
  For a butcher fain would I be."

"The price of my flesh," the butcher repli'd,
  "I soon will tell unto thee;
With my bonny mare, and they are not too dear,
  Four mark thou must give unto me."

"Four mark I will give thee," saith jolly Robin,
  "Four mark it shall be thy fee;
The mony come count, and let me mount,
  For a butcher I fain would be."

Now Robin he is to Nottingham gone,
  His butchers trade to begin;
With good intent to the sheriff he went,
  And there he took up his inn.

When other butchers did open their meat,
  Bold Robin he then begun;
But how for to sell he knew not well,
  For a butcher he was but young.

When other butchers no meat could sell,
  Robin got both gold and fee;
For he sold more meat for one peny
  Then others could do for three.

But when he sold his meat so fast,
  No butcher by him could thrive;
For he sold more meat for one peny
  Than others could do for five.

Which made the butchers of Nottingham
  To study as they did stand,
Saying, "Surely he 'is' some prodigal,
  That hath sold his fathers land."

The butchers stepped to jolly Robin,
  Acquainted with him for to be;
"Come, brother," one said, "we be all of
    one trade,
  Come, will you go dine with me?"

"Accurst of his heart," said jolly Robin,
  "That a butcher doth deny;
I will go with you, my brethren true,
  As fast as I can hie."

But when to the sheriffs house they came,
  To dinner they hied apace,
And Robin Hood he the man must be
  Before them all to say grace.

"Pray God bless us all," said jolly Robin,
  "And our meat within this place;
A cup of sack so good will nourish our blood,
  And so do I end my grace."

"Come fill us more wine," said jolly Robin,
  "Let us be merry while we do stay;
For wine and good cheer, be it never so dear,
  I vow I the reck'ning will pay.

"Come, 'brothers,' be merry," said jolly
    Robin,
  "Let us drink, and never give ore;
For the shot I will pay, ere I go my way,
  If it cost me five pounds and more."

"This is a mad blade," the butchers then said;
  Saies the sheriff, "He is some prodigal,
That some land has sold for silver and gold,
  And now he doth mean to spend all.

"Hast thou any horn beasts," the sheriff repli'd,
  "Good fellow, to sell unto me?"
"Yes, that I have, good master sheriff,
  I have hundreds two or three;

"And a hundred aker of good free land,
  If you please it to see:
And Ile make you as good assurance of it,
  As ever my father made me."

The sheriff he saddled his good palfrèy,
  And, with three hundred pound in gold,
Away he went with bold Robin Hood,
  His horned beasts to behold.

Away then the sheriff and Robin did ride,
  To the forrest of merry Sherwood;
Then the sheriff did say, "God bless us this day
  From a man they call Robin Hood!"

But when a little farther they came,
  Bold Robin he chancèd to spy
A hundred head of good red deer,
  Come tripping the sheriff full nigh.

"How like you my horn'd beasts, good master sheriff?
  They be fat and fair for to see;"
"I tell thee, good fellow, I would I were gone,
  For I like not thy company."

Then Robin set his horn to his mouth,
  And blew but blasts three;
Then quickly anon there came Little John,
  And all his company.

"What is your will, master?" then said Little John,
"Good master come tell unto me;"
"I have brought hither the sheriff of Nottingham
This day to dine with thee."

"He is welcome to me," then said Little John,
"I hope he will honestly pay;
I know he has gold, if it be but well told,
Will serve us to drink a whole day."

Then Robin took his mantle from his back,
And laid it upon the ground:
And out of the sheriffs portmantle
He told three hundred pound.

Then Robin he brought him thorow the wood,
And set him on his dapple gray;
"O have me commended to your wife at home;"
So Robin went laughing away.

NOTES

NOTES

Sir Patrick Spens.—p. 1.

Mr. Child finds the first published version of "the grand old ballad of Sir Patrick Spens," as Coleridge calls it, in Bishop Percy's *Reliques*. Here the name is "Spence," and the middle rhyme—

"Haf owre, haf owre to Aberdour,"

is not of early date. The "Cork-heeled Shoon," too, cannot be early, but ballads are subject, in oral tradition, to such modern interpolations. The verse about the ladies waiting vainly is anticipated in a popular song of the fourteenth century, on a defeat of the *noblesse* in Flanders—

"Their ladies them may abide in bower and hall well long!"

If there be historical foundation for the ballad, it is probably a blending of the voyage of Margaret, daughter of Alexander III., to wed Eric, King of Norway, in 1281 (some of her escort were drowned on their way home), with the rather mysterious death, or disappearance, of Margaret's daughter, "The Maid of Norway," on her voyage to marry the son of Edward I., in 1290. A woman, who alleged that she was the Maid of Norway, was later burned at the stake. The great number and variety of versions sufficiently indicate the antiquity of this ballad, wherein exact history is not to be expected.

Notes

THE BATTLE OF OTTERBURN.—p. 5.

From *The Border Minstrelsy*, Sir Walter Scott's latest edition of 1833: the copy in the edition of 1802 is less complete. The gentle and joyous passage of arms here recorded, took place in August 1388. We have an admirable account of Otterburn fight from Froissart, who revels in a gallant encounter, fairly fought out hand to hand, with no intervention of archery or artillery, and for no wretched practical purpose. In such a combat the Scots, never renowned for success at long bowls, and led by a Douglas, were likely to prove victorious, even against long odds, and when taken by surprise. Choosing an advantage in the discordant days of Richard II., the Scots mustered a very large force near Jedburgh, merely to break lances on English ground, and take loot. Learning that, as they advanced by the Carlisle route, the English intended to invade Scotland by Berwick and the east coast, the Scots sent three or four hundred men-at-arms, with a few thousand mounted archers and pikemen, who should harry Northumberland to the walls of Newcastle. These were led by James, Earl of Douglas, March, and Murray. In a fight at Newcastle, Douglas took Harry Percy's pennon, which Hotspur vowed to recover. The retreat began, but the Scots waited at Otterburn, partly to besiege the castle, partly to abide Hotspur's challenge. He made his attack by moonlight, with overwhelming odds, but was hampered by a marsh, and incommoded by a flank attack of the Scots. Then it came to who would pound longest, with axe and sword. Douglas cut his way through the English, axe in hand, and was overthrown, but his men protected his body. The Sinclairs and Lindsay raised his banner, with his cry; March and Dunbar came up; Hotspur was taken by Montgomery, and the English were routed with heavy loss. Douglas was buried in Melrose Abbey; very many years later the English defiled his grave, but were punished at Ancram Moor. There is an English poem on the fight of "about 1550"; it has many analogies with our Scottish version, and, doubtless, ours descends from a ballad almost contemporary. The ballad was a great favourite of Scott's. In a severe illness, thinking of Lockhart, not yet his son-in-law, he quoted—

> "My wound is deep, I fain would sleep,
> Take thou the vanguard of the three."

Mr. Child thinks the command to

> "yield to the bracken-bush"

unmartial. This does not seem a strong objection, in Froissart's time. It is explained in an oral fragment—

> "For there lies aneth yon bracken-bush
> Wha aft has conquered mair than thee."

Mr. Child also thinks that the "dreary dream" may be copied from Hume of Godscroft. It is at least as probable that Godscroft borrowed from the ballad which he cites. The embroidered gauntlet of the Percy is in the possession of Douglas of Cavers to this day.

TAM LIN, OR TAMLANE.—p. 10.

Burns's version, in Johnson's *Museum* (1792). Scott's version is made up of this copy, Riddell's, Herd's, and oral recitations, and contains feeble literary interpolations, not, of course, by Sir Walter. *The Complaint of Scotland* (1549) mentions the "Tale of the Young Tamlene" as then popular. It is needless here to enter into the subject of Fairyland, and captures of mortals by Fairies; the Editor has said his say in his edition of Kirk's *Secret Commonwealth*. The Nereids, in Modern Greece, practise fairy cantrips, and the same beliefs exist in Samoa and New Caledonia. The metamorphoses are found in the *Odyssey*, Book iv., in the winning of Thetis, the *Nereid, or Fairy Bride*, by Peleus, in a modern Cretan fairy tale, and so on. There is a similar incident in *Penda Baloa*, a Senegambian ballad (*Contes Populaires de la Sénégambie*, Berenger Ferand, Paris, 1885). The dipping of Tamlane has precedents in *Old Deccan Days*, in a Hottentot tale by Bleek, and in *Les Deux Frères*, the Egyptian story, translated by Maspero (the Editor has already given these parallels in a note to *Border Ballads*, by Graham R. Tomson). Mr. Child also cites Mannhardt, "Wald und Feldkulte," ii. 64-70.

Carterhaugh, the scene of the ballad, is at the junction of Ettrick and Yarrow, between Bowhill and Philiphaugh.

THOMAS RYMER.—p. 16.

From *The Border Minstrelsy*; the original was derived from a lady living near Erceldoune (Earlston), and from Mrs. Brown's MSS. That Thomas of Erceldoune had some popular fame as a rhymer and soothsayer as early as 1320-1350, seems to be established. As late as the Forty Five, nay, even as late as the expected Napoleonic invasion, sayings attributed to Thomas were repeated with some measure of belief. A real Thomas Rymer of Erceldoune witnessed an undated deed of Peter de Haga, early in the thirteenth century. The de Hagas, or Haigs of Bemersyde, were the subjects of the prophecy attributed to Thomas,

"Betide, betide, whate'er betide,
There will aye be a Haig in Bemersyde,"

and a Haig still owns that ancient *château* on the Tweed, which has a singular set of traditions. Learmont is usually given as the Erceldoune family name; a branch of the family owned Dairsie in Fifeshire, and were a kind of hereditary provosts of St. Andrews. If Thomas did predict the death of Alexander III., or rather report it by dint of clairvoyance, he must have lived till 1296. The date of the poem on the Fairy Queen, attributed to Thomas, is uncertain, the story itself is a variant of "Ogier the Dane." The scene is Huntly Bank, under Eildon Hill, and was part of the lands acquired, at fantastic prices, by Sir Walter Scott. His passion for land was really part of his passion for collecting antiquities. The theory of Fairyland here (as in many other Scottish legends and witch trials) is borrowed from the Pre-Christian Hades, and the Fairy Queen is a late refraction from Persephone. Not to eat, in the realm of the dead, is a regular precept of savage belief, all the world over. Mr. Robert Kirk's *Secret Commonwealth of Elves, Fauns, and Fairies* may be consulted, or the Editor's *Perrault*, p. xxxv. (Oxford, 1888). Of the later legends about Thomas, Scott gives plenty, in *The Border Minstrelsy*. The long ancient romantic poem on the subject is probably the source of the ballad, though a local ballad may have preceded the long poem. Scott named the glen through which the Bogle Burn flows to Chiefswood, "The Rhymer's Glen."

Sir Hugh.—p. 19.

The date of the Martyrdom of Hugh is attributed by Matthew Paris to 1225. Chaucer puts a version in the mouth of his Prioress. No doubt the story must have been a mere excuse for Jew-baiting. In America the Jew becomes "The Duke" in a version picked up by Mr. Newells, from the recitation of a street boy in New York. The daughter of a Jew is not more likely than the daughter of a duke to have been concerned in the cruel and blasphemous imitation of the horrors attributed by Horace to the witch Canidia. But some such survivals of pagan sorcery did survive in the Middle Ages, under the influence of "Satanism."

Son Davie.—p. 22.

Motherwell's version. One of many ballads on fratricide, instigated by the mother: or inquired into by her, as the case may be. "Edward" is another example of this gloomy situation.

The Wife of Usher's Well.—p. 24.

Here

"The cock doth craw, the day doth daw,"

having a middle rhyme, can scarcely be of extreme antiquity. Probably, in the original poem, the dead return to rebuke the extreme grief of the Mother, but the poem is perhaps really more affecting in the absence of a didactic motive. Scott obtained it from an old woman in West Lothian. Probably the reading "fashes" (troubles), "in the flood" is correct, not "fishes," or "freshes." The mother desires that the sea may never cease to be troubled till her sons return (verse 4, line 2). The peculiar doom of women dead in child-bearing occurs even in Aztec mythology.

Notes

THE TWA CORBIES.—p. 26.

From the third volume of *Border Minstrelsy*, derived by Charles Kirkpatrick Sharpe from a traditional version. The English version, "Three Ravens," was published in *Melismata*, by T. Ravensworth (1611). In Scots, the lady "has ta'en another mate" his hawk and hound have deserted the dead knight. In the English song, the hounds watch by him, the hawks keep off carrion birds, as for the lady—

"She buried him before the prime,
  She was dead herselfe ere evensong time."

Probably the English is the earlier version.

THE BONNIE EARL OF MURRAY.—p. 27.

Huntly had a commission to apprehend the Earl, who was in the disgrace of James VI. Huntly, as an ally of Bothwell, asked him to surrender at Donibristle, in Fife; he would not yield to his private enemy, the house was burned, and Murray was slain, Huntly gashing his face. "You have spoiled a better face than your own," said the dying Earl (1592). James Melville mentions contemporary ballads on the murder. Ramsay published the ballad in his *Tea Table Miscellany*, and it is often sung to this day.

CLERK SAUNDERS.—p. 30.

First known as published in *Border Minstrelsy* (1802). The apparition of the lover is borrowed from "Sweet Willie's Ghost." The evasions practised by the lady, and the austerities vowed by her have many Norse, French, and Spanish parallels in folk-poetry. Scott's version is "made up" from several sources, but is, in any case, verse most satisfactory as poetry.

WALY, WALY.—p. 35.

From Ramsay's *Tea Table Miscellany*, a curiously composite gathering of verses. There is a verse, obviously a variant, in a sixteenth century song, cited by

Leyden. St. Anthon's Well is on a hill slope of Arthur's Seat, near Holyrood. Here Jeanie Deans trysted with her sister's seducer, in *The Heart of Midlothian*. The Cairn of Nichol Mushat, the wife-murderer, is not far off. The ruins of Anthony's Chapel are still extant.

LOVE GREGOR.—p. 37.

There are French and Romaic variants of this ballad. "Lochroyal," where the ballad is localized, is in Wigtownshire, but the localization varies. The "tokens" are as old as the Return of Odysseus, in the *Odyssey*: his token is the singular construction of his bridal bed, attached by him to a living tree-trunk. A similar legend occurs in Chinese. See Gerland's *Alt-Griechische Märchen*.

THE QUEEN'S MARIE—MARY HAMILTON.—p. 41.

A made-up copy from Scott's edition of 1833. This ballad has caused a great deal of controversy. Queen Mary had no Mary Hamilton among her Four Maries. No Marie was executed for child-murder. But we know, from Knox, that ballads were recited against the Maries, and that one of Mary's chamberwomen was hanged, with her lover, a pottinger, or apothecary, for getting rid of her infant. These last facts were certainly quite basis enough for a ballad, the ballad echoing, not history, but rumour, and rumour adapted to the popular taste. Thus the ballad might have passed unchallenged, as a survival, more or less modified in time, of Queen Mary's period. But in 1719 a Mary Hamilton, a Maid of Honour, of Scottish descent, was executed in Russia, for infanticide. Charles Kirkpatrick Sharpe conceived that this affair was the origin of the ballad, and is followed by Mr. Child.

We reply (1) The ballad has almost the largest number of variants on record. This is a proof of antiquity. Variants so many, differing in all sorts of points, could not have arisen between 1719, and the age of Burns, who quotes the poem.

(2) This is especially improbable, because, in 1719, the old vein of ballad poetry had run dry, popular song

had chosen other forms, and no literary imitator could have written Mary Hamilton in 1719.

(3) There is no example of a popular ballad in which a contemporary event, interesting just because it is contemporary, is thrown back into a remote age.

(4) The name, Mary Hamilton, is often *not* given to the heroine in variants of the ballad. She is of several names and ranks in the variants.

(5) As Mr. Child himself remarked, the "pottinger" of the real story of Queen Mary's time occurs in one variant. There was no "pottinger" in the Russian affair.

All these arguments, to which others might be added, seem fatal to the late date and modern origin of the ballad, and Mr. Child's own faith in the hypothesis was shaken, if not overthrown.

KINMONT WILLIE.—p. 45.

From *The Border Minstrelsy*. The account in Satchells has either been based on the ballad, or the ballad is based on Satchells. After a meeting, on the Border of Salkeld of Corby, and Scott of Haining, Kinmont Willie was seized by the English as he rode home from the tryst. Being "wanted," he was lodged in Carlisle Castle, and this was a breach of the day's truce. Buccleugh, as warder, tried to obtain Willie's release by peaceful means. These failing, Buccleugh did what the ballad reports, April 13, 1596. Harden and Goudilands were with Buccleugh, being his neighbours near Branxholme. Dicky of Dryhope, with others, Armstrongs, was also true to the call of duty. A few verses in the ballad are clearly by *aut Gualterus aut diabolus*, and none the worse for that. Salkeld, of course, was not really slain; and, if the men were "left for dead," probably they were not long in that debatable condition. In the rising of 1745 Prince Charlie's men forded Eden as boldly as Buccleuch, the Prince saving a drowning Highlander with his own hand.

JAMIE TELFER.—p. 52.

Scott, for once, was wrong in his localities. The Dodhead of the poem is *not* that near Singlee, in

Ettrick, but a place of the same name, near Skelfhill, on the southern side of Teviot, within three miles of Stobs, where Telfer vainly seeks help from Elliot. The other Dodhead is at a great distance from Stobs, up Borthwick Water, over the tableland, past Clearburn Loch and Buccleugh, and so down Ettrick, past Tushielaw. The Catslockhill is not that on Yarrow, near Ladhope, but another near Branxholme, whence it is no far cry to Branxholme Hall. Borthwick Water, Goudilands (below Branxholme), Commonside (a little farther up Teviot), Allanhaugh, and the other places of the Scotts, were all easily "warned." There are traces of a modern hand in this excellent ballad. The topography is here corrected from MS. notes in a first edition of the *Minstrelsy*, in the library of Mr. Charles Grieve at Branxholme Park, a scion of "auld Jock Grieve" of the Coultart Cleugh. Names linger long in pleasant Teviotdale.

THE DOUGLAS TRAGEDY.—p. 59.

The ballad has Norse analogues, but is here localized on the Douglas Burn, a tributary of Yarrow, on the left bank. The St. Mary's Kirk would be that now ruinous, on St. Mary's Loch, the chapel burned by the Lady of Branxholme when she

"gathered a band
Of the best that would ride at her command,"

in the *Lay of the Last Minstrel*. The ancient keep of Blackhouse on Douglas Burn may have been the home of the heroine, if we are to localize.

THE BONNY HIND.—p. 62.

Herd got this tragic ballad from a milkmaid, in 1771. Mr. Child quotes a verse parallel, preserved in Faroe, and in the Icelandic. There is a similar incident in the cycle of Kullervo, in the Finnish *Kalevala*. Scott says that similar tragedies are common in Scotch popular poetry; such cases are "Lizzie Wan," and "The King's Dochter, Lady Jean." A sorrow nearly as bitter occurs in the French "Milk White Dove": a brother kills his sister, metamorphosed into a white deer. "The Bridge of Death" (French) seems to hint at something of the same kind; or rather the Editor finds that he has arbitrarily read "The Bonny Hind" into "Le Pont des Morts," in Puymaigre's *Chants Populaires du Pays Messin*, p. 60. (*Ballads and Lyrics of Old France*, p. 63.)

YOUNG BEICHAN, OR YOUNG BICHAM.—p. 65.

This is the original of the Cockney *Loving Ballad of Lord Bateman*, illustrated by Cruikshank, and by Thackeray. There is a vast number of variants, evidence to the antiquity of the story. The earliest known trace is in the familiar legend of the Saracen lady, who sought and found her lover, Gilbert Becket, father of Thomas à Becket, in London (see preface to *Life of Becket*, or Beket), Percy Society, 1845. The date may be *circ.* 1300. The kind of story, the loving daughter of the cruel captor, is as old as Medea and Jason, and her search for her lover comes in such *Märchen* as "The Black Bull o' Norraway." No story is more widely diffused (see *A Far Travelled Tale*, in the Editor's *Custom and Myth*). The appearance of the "True Love," just at her lover's wedding, is common in the *Märchen* of the world, and occurs in a Romaic ballad, as well as in many from Northern Europe. The "local colour"—the Moor or Saracen—is derived from Crusading times, perhaps. Motherwell found the ballad recited with intervals of prose narrative, as in *Aucassin and Nicolette*. The notes to Cruikshank's *Loving Ballad* are, obviously, by Thackeray.

THE BONNY HOUSE O' AIRLY.—p. 73.

Lord Airly's houses were destroyed by Argyll, representing the Covenanters, and also in pursuance of a private feud, in 1639, or 1640. There are erroneous versions of this ballad, in which Lochiel appears, and the date is, apparently, transferred to 1745. Montrose, in his early Covenanting days, was not actually concerned in the burning of the Bonnie House, which he, when a Royalist, revenged on the possessions of "gleyed Argyll." The reference to "Charlie" is out of keeping; no one, perhaps, ever called Charles I.

by that affectionate name. Lady Ogilvie had not the large family attributed to her: her son, Lord Ogilvie, escaped from prison in the Castle of St. Andrews, after Philiphaugh. A Lord Ogilvie was out in 1745, and, later, had a regiment in the French Service. Few families have a record so consistently loyal.

ROB ROY.—p. 75.

The abductors of the widowed young heiress of Edenhelly were Rob's sons, Robin Oig, who went through a form of marriage with the girl, and James Mohr, a good soldier, but a double-dyed spy and scoundrel. Robin Oig was hanged in 1753. James Mohr, a detected traitor to Prince Charles, died miserably in Paris, in 1754. Readers of Mr. Stevenson's *Catriona* know James well; information as to his villanies is extant in Additional MSS. (British Museum). This is probably the latest ballad in the collection. It occurs in several variants, some of which, copied out by Burns, derive thence a certain accidental interest. In Mr. Stevenson's *Catriona*, the heroine of that name takes a thoroughly Highland view of the abduction. Robin Oig, in any case, was "nane the waur o' a hanging," for he shot a Maclaren at the plough-tail, before the Forty-Five. The trial of these sons of Alpen was published shortly after Scott's *Rob Roy*.

KILLIECRANKIE.—p. 77.

Fought on July 27, 1689. *Not* on the haugh near the modern road by the railway, but higher up the hill, in the grounds of Urrard House. Two shelter trenches, whence Dundee's men charged, are still visible, high on the hillside above Urrard. There is said, by Mr. Child, to have been a contemporary broadside of the ballad, which is an example of the evolution of popular ballads from the old traditional model. There is another song, by, or attributed to, Burns, and of remarkable spirit and vigour.

ANNAN WATER.—p. 79.

'From *The Border Minstrelsy*. Scott says that these are the original words of the tune of "Allan Water," and that he has added two verses from a variant with a fortunate conclusion. "Allan Water" is a common river name; the stream so called joins Teviot above Branxholme. Annan is the large stream that flows into the Solway Frith. The Gate-slack, in Annandale, fixes the locality.

THE ELPHIN NOURRICE.—p. 81.

This curious poem is taken from the reprint of Charles Kirkpatrick Sharpe's tiny *Ballad Book*, itself now almost *introuvable*. It does not, to the Editor's knowledge, occur elsewhere, but is probably authentic. The view of the Faery Queen is more pleasing and sympathetic than usual. Why mortal women were desired as nurses (except to attend on stolen mortal children, kept to "pay the Kane to hell") is not obvious. Irish beliefs are precisely similar; in England they are of frequent occurrence.

JOHNNIE ARMSTRANG.—p. 87.

Armstrang of Gilnockie was a brother of the laird of Mangertoun. He had a kind of Robin Hood reputation on the Scottish Border, as one who only robbed the English. Pitscottie's account of his slaying by James V. (1529) reads as if the ballad were his authority, and an air for the subject is mentioned in the *Complaint of Scotland*. In Sir Herbert Maxwell's *History of Dumfries and Galloway* is an excellent account of the historical facts of the case.

EDOM O' GORDON.—p. 92.

Founded on an event in the wars between Kingsmen and Queensmen, in the minority of James VI., while Queen Mary was imprisoned in England. "Edom" was Adam Gordon of Auchindown, brother of Huntley, and a Queen's man. He, by his retainer, Car, or Ker, burned Towie House, a seat of the Forbes's. Ker recurs in the long and more or less literary ballad of *The Battle of Balrinnes*. In variants the localities are much altered, and, in one version, the scene is transferred to Ayrshire, and Loudoun Castle. All the ballads of fire-raising, a very usual practice, have points in common, and transference was easy.

LADY ANNE BOTHWELL'S LAMENT.—p. 98.

Tradition has confused the heroine of this piece with the wife of Bothwelhaugh, who slew the Regent Murray. That his motive was not mere political assassination, but to avenge the ill-treatment and death of his wife, seems to be disproved by Maidment. The affair, however, is still obscure. This deserted Lady Anne of the ballad was, in fact, not the wife of Bothwelhaugh, but the daughter of the Bishop of Orkney; her lover is said to have been her cousin, Alexander Erskine, son of the Earl of Mar. Part of the poem (Mr. Child points out) occurs in Broome's play, *The Northern Lass* (1632). Though a popular favourite, the piece is clearly of literary origin, and has been severely "edited" by a literary hand. This version is Allan Ramsay's.

JOCK O' THE SIDE.—p. 101.

A Liddesdale chant. Jock flourished about 1550-1570, and is commemorated as a reiver by Sir Richard Maitland in a poem often quoted. The analogies of this ballad with that of "Kinmont Willie" are very close. The reference to a punch-bowl sounds modern, and the tale is much less plausible than that of "Kinmont Willie," which, however, bears a few obvious marks of Sir Walter's own hand. A sceptical editor must choose between two theories: either Scott of Satchells founded his account of the affair of "Kinmont Willie" on a pre-existing ballad of that name, or the ballad printed by Scott is based on the prose narrative of Scott of Satchells. The former hypothesis, everything considered, is the more probable.

Notes

LORD THOMAS AND FAIR ANNET.—p. 107.

Published in Percy's *Reliques*, from a Scotch manuscript, "with some corrections." The situation, with various differences in detail and conclusion, is popular in Norse and Romaic ballads, and also in many *Märchen* of the type of *The Black Bull of Norraway*.

FAIR ANNIE.—p. 111.

From *The Border Minstrelsy*. There are Danish, Swedish, Dutch, and German versions, and the theme enters artistic poetry as early as Marie de France (*Le Lai del Freisne*). In Scotch the Earl of Wemyss is a recent importation: the earldom dates from 1633. Of course this process of attaching a legend or *Märchen* to a well-known name, or place, is one of the most common in mythological evolution, and by itself invalidates the theory which would explain myths by a philological analysis of the proper names in the tale. These may not be, and probably are not, the original names.

THE DOWIE DENS OF YARROW.—p. 116.

From *The Border Minstrelsy*. Scott thought that the hero was Walter Scott, third son of Thirlestane, slain by Scott of Tushielaw. The "monument" (a standing stone near Yarrow) is really of a very early, rather post-Roman date, and refers to no feud of Thirlestane, Oakwood, Kirkhope, or Tushielaw. The stone is not far from Yarrow Kirk, near a place called Warrior's Rest. Hamilton of Bangour's version is beautiful and well known. Quite recently a very early interment of a corpse, in the curved position, was discovered not far from the standing stone with the inscription. Ballad, stone, and interment may all be distinct and separate.

SIR ROLAND.—p. 119.

From Motherwell's *Minstrelsy*. The authenticity of the ballad is dubious, but, if a forgery, it is a very skilled one for the early nineteenth century. Poets like Mr. Swinburne, Mr. Rossetti, and Mrs. Marriot Watson have imitated the genuine popular ballad, but never so closely as the author of "Sir Roland."

ROSE THE RED AND WHITE LILY.—p. 123.

From the Jamieson-Brown MS., originally written out by Mrs. Brown in 1783: Sir Walter made changes in *The Border Minstrelsy*. The ballad is clearly a composite affair. Robert Chambers regarded Mrs. Brown as the Mrs. Harris of ballad lore, but Mr. Norval Clyne's reply was absolutely crushing and satisfactory.

THE BATTLE OF HARLAW.—p. 131.

Fought on July 24, 1411. This fight broke the Highland force in Scotland. The first version is, of course, literary, perhaps a composition of 1550, or even earlier. The second version is traditional, and was procured by Aytoun from Lady John Scott, herself the author of some beautiful songs. But the best ballad on the Red Harlaw is that placed by Scott in the mouth of Elspeth, in *The Antiquary*. This, indeed, is beyond all rivalry the most splendid modern imitation of the ancient popular Muse.

DICKIE MACPHALION.—p. 142.

A great favourite of Scott's, who heard it sung at Miss Edgeworth's, during his tour in Ireland (1825). One verse recurs in a Jacobite chant, probably of 1745-1760, but the bibliography of Jacobite songs is especially obscure.

A LYKE-WAKE DIRGE.—p. 143.

From the *Border Minstrelsy*. The ideas are mainly pre-Christian; the Brig o' Dread occurs in Islamite and Iroquois belief, and in almost all mythologies the souls have to cross a River. Music for this dirge is given in Mr. Harold Boulton's and Miss Macleod's *Songs of the North*.

THE LAIRD OF WARISTOUN.—p. 145.

This version was taken down by Sir Walter Scott from his mother's recitation, for Jamieson's book of ballads. Jamieson later quarrelled bitterly with Sir Walter, as letters at Abbotsford prove. A variant is given by Kinloch, and a longer, less poetical, but more historically accurate version is given by Buchan. The House of Waristoun is, or lately was, a melancholy place hanging above a narrow lake, in the northern suburbs of Edinburgh, near the Water of Leith. Kincaid was the name of the Laird; according to Chambers, the more famous lairds of Covenanting times were Johnstons. Kincaid is said to have treated his wife cruelly, wherefore she, or her nurse, engaged one Robert Weir, an old servant of her father (Livingstone of Dunipace), to strangle the unhappy man in his own bedroom (July 2, 1600). The lady was beheaded, the nurse was burned, and, later, Weir was also executed. The line

"I wish that ye may sink for sin"

occurs in an earlier ballad on Edinburgh Castle—

"And that all for the black dinner
Earl Douglas got therein."

MAY COLVEN.—p. 147.

From Herd's MS. Versions occur in Polish, German, Magyar, Portuguese, Scandinavian, and in French. The ballad is here localised on the Carrick coast, near Girvan. The lady is regarded as a Kennedy of Culzean. Prof. Bugge regards this widely diffused ballad as based on the Apocryphal legend of Judith and Holofernes. If so, the legend is *diablement changé en route*. More probably the origin is a *Märchen* of a kind of *Rakshasa* fatal to women. Mr. Child has collected a vast mass of erudition on the subject, and by no means acquiesces in Prof. Bugge's ingenious hypothesis.

JOHNIE FAA.—p. 150.

From Pinkerton's Scottish Ballads. The event narrated is a legend of the house of Cassilis (Kennedy), but is wholly unhistorical. "Sir John Faa," in the fable, is aided by Gypsies, but, apparently, is not one of the Earls of Egypt, on whom Mr. Crockett's novel, *The Raiders*, may be consulted. The ballad was first printed, as far as is known, in Ramsay's *Tea Table Miscellany*.

HOBBIE NOBLE.—p. 152.

The hero recurs in *Jock o' the Side*, and Jock o' the Mains is an historical character, that is, finds mention in authentic records, as Scott points out. The Armstrongs were deported in great numbers, as "an ill colony," to Ulster, by James I. Sir Herbert Maxwell's *History of Dumfries and Galloway* may be consulted for these and similar reivers.

THE TWA SISTERS.—p. 157.

A version of "Binnorie." The ballad here ends abruptly; doubtless the fiddler made fiddle-strings of the lady's hair, and a fiddle of her breast-bone, while the instrument probably revealed the cruelty of the sister. Other extant versions are composite or interpolated, so this fragment (Sharpe's) has been preferred in this place.

MARY AMBREE.—p. 160.

Taken by Percy from a piece in the Pepys Collection. The girl warrior is a favourite figure in popular romance. Often she slays a treacherous lover, as in *Billy Taylor*. Nothing is known of Mary Ambree as an historical personage; she may be as legendary as fair maiden Lilias, of Liliard's Edge, who "fought upon her stumps." In that case the local name is demonstrably earlier than the mythical Lilias, who fought with such tenacity.

ALISON GROSS.—p. 165.

Jamieson gave this ballad from a manuscript, altering the spelling in conformity with Scots orthography. Mr. Child prints the manuscript; here Jamieson's more familiar spelling is retained. The idea of the romance occurs in a Romaic *Märchen*, but, in place of the Queen of Faery, a more beautiful girl than the sorceress (Nereid in Romaic), restores the youth to his true shape. Mr. Child regarded the tale as "one of the numerous wild growths" from *Beauty and the Beast*. It would be more correct to say that *Beauty and the Beast* is a late, courtly, French adaptation and amplification of the original popular "wild growth" which first appears (in literary form) as *Cupid and Psyche*, in Apuleius. Except for the metamorphosis, however, there is little analogy in this case. The friendly act of the Fairy Queen is without parallel in British Folklore, but Mr. Child points out that the Nereid Queen, in Greece, is still as kind as Thetis of old, not a sepulchral siren, the shadow of the pagan "Fairy Queen Proserpina," as Campion calls her.

THE HEIR OF LYNNE.—p. 167.

From Percy's Folio Manuscript. There is a cognate Greek epigram—

Χρυσὸν ἀνὴς εὑρων ἔλιπε βρόχον αὐτὰρ ὁ χρυσόν
Ὅν λίπεν, οὐχ εὑρών, ἧψεν τὸν εὗρε βρόχον.

GORDON OF BRACKLEY.—p. 172.

This, though probably not the most authentic, is decidedly the most pleasing version; it is from Mackay's collection, perhaps from his pen.

EDWARD.—p. 175.

Percy got this piece from Lord Hailes, with pseudo-antiquated spelling. Mr. Swinburne has published a parallel ballad "From the Finnish." There are a number of parallel ballads on Cruel Brothers, and Cruel Sisters, such as *Son Davie*, which may be compared. Fratricides and unconscious incests were motives dear to popular poetry.

YOUNG BENJIE.—p. 177.

From the *Border Minstrelsy*. That corpses *might* begin to "thraw," if carelessly watched, was a prevalent superstition. Scott gives an example: the following may be added, as less well known. The watchers had left the corpse alone, and were dining in the adjoining room, when a terrible noise was heard in the chamber of death. None dared enter; the minister was sent for, and passed into the room. He emerged, asked for a pair of tongs, and returned, bearing in the tongs *a bloody glove*, and the noise ceased. He always declined to say what he had witnessed. Ministers were exorcists in the last century, and the father of James Thomson, the poet, died suddenly in an interview with a guest, in a haunted house. The house was pulled down, as being uninhabitable.

AULD MAITLAND.—p. 180.

From *The Border Minstrelsy*. This ballad is inserted, not for its merit, still less for its authenticity, but for the problem of its puzzling history. Scott certainly got it from the mother of the Ettrick Shepherd, in 1801. The Shepherd's father had been a grown-up man in 1745, and his mother also was of great age, and unlikely to be able to learn a new-forged ballad by heart. The Shepherd himself (then a most unsophisticated person) said, in a letter of June 30, 1801, that he was "surprised to hear this song is suspected by some to be a modern forgery; the contrary will be best proved by most of the old people, here about, having a great part of it by heart." The two last lines of verse seven were, confessedly, added by Hogg, to fill a *lacuna*. They are especially modern in style. Now thus to fill up sham *lacunæ* in sham ballads of his own, with lines manifestly modern, was a favourite trick of Surtees of Mainsforth. He used the device in "Barthram's Dirge," which entirely took in Sir Walter, and was guilty of many other *supercheries*, especially of the "Fray of Suport Mill." Could the unlettered Shepherd, fond of hoaxes as he was, have invented this stratagem, sixteen years before he joined the *Blackwood* set? And is it conceivable that his old mother, entering into the joke, would commit her son's fraudulent verses to memory, and recite them to Sir Walter as genuine tradition? She said to Scott, that the ballad "never was printed i' the world, for my brothers and me learned it and many mae frae auld Andrew Moore, and he learned it frae auld Baby Mettlin" (Maitland?) "wha was housekeeper to the first laird o' Tushilaw." (On Ettrick, near Thirlestane. She doubtless meant the first of the Andersons of Tushielaw, who succeeded the old lairds, the Scotts.) "She was said to hae been another or a guid ane, and there are many queer stories about hersel', but O, she had been a grand singer o' auld songs an' ballads." (Hogg's *Domestic Manners of Sir Walter Scott*, p. 61, 1834.)

"Maitland upon auld beird gray" is mentioned by Gawain Douglas, in his *Palice of Honour*, which the Shepherd can hardly have read, and Scott identified this Maitland with the ancestor of Lethington; his date was 1250-1296. On the whole, even the astute Shepherd, in his early days of authorship, could hardly have laid a plot so insidious, and the question of the authenticity and origin of the ballad (obvious interpolations apart) remains a mystery. Who could have forged it? It is, as an exercise in imitation, far beyond *Hardyknute*, and at least on a level with *Sir Roland*. The possibility of such forgeries is now very slight indeed, but vitiates early collections.

If we suspect Leyden, who alone had the necessary knowledge of antiquities, we are still met by the improbability of old Mrs. Hogg being engaged in the hoax. Moreover, Leyden was probably too keen an antiquary to take part in one of the deceptions which Ritson wished to punish so severely. Mr. Child expresses his strong and natural suspicions of the authenticity of the ballad, and Hogg is, certainly, a dubious source. He took in Jeffrey with the song of "Donald Macgillavray," and instantly boasted of his triumph. He could not have kept his secret, after the death of Scott. These considerations must not be neglected, however suspicious "Auld Maitland" may appear.

THE BROOMFIELD HILL.—p. 189.

From Buchan's *Ballads of the North of Scotland*. There are Elizabethan references to the poem, and a twelfth century romance turns on the main idea of sleep magically induced. The lover therein is more fortunate than the hero of the ballad, and, finally, overcomes the spell. The idea recurs in the Norse poetry.

WILLIE'S LADYE.—p. 193.

Scott took this ballad from Mrs. Brown's celebrated Manuscript. The kind of spell indicated was practised by Hera upon Alcmena, before the birth of Heracles. Analogous is the spell by binding witch-knots, practised by Simaetha on her lover, in the second Idyll of Theocritus. Montaigne has some curious remarks on these enchantments, explaining their power by what is now called "suggestion." There is a Danish parallel to "Willie's Ladye," translated by Jamieson.

ROBIN HOOD BALLADS.—p. 196.

There is plentiful "learning" about Robin Hood, but no real knowledge. He is first mentioned in literature, as the subject of "rhymes," in *Piers Plowman* (*circ.* 1377). As a topic of ballads he must be much older than that date. In 1439 his name was a synonym for a bandit. Wyntoun, the Scots chronicler, dates the outlaw in the time of Edward I. Major, the Scots philosopher and master of John Knox, makes a guess (taken up by Scott in *Ivanhoe*) at the period of Richard I. Kuhn seeks to show that Hood is a survival of Woden, or of his *Wooden*, "wooden horse," or hobby horse. The Robin Hood play was parallel with the May games, which, as Mr. Frazer shows in his *Golden Bough*, were really survivals of a world-wide religious practice. But Robin Hood need not be confused with the legendary May King. Mr. Child judiciously rejects these mythological conjectures, based, as they are, on far-fetched etymologies and analogies. Robin is an idealized bandit, reiver, or Klepht, as in modern Romaic ballads, and his adventures are precisely such as popular fancy everywhere attaches to such popular heroes. An historical Robin there may have been, but *premit nox alta*.

ROBIN HOOD AND THE MONK.—p. 196.

This copy follows in Mr. Child's early edition, "from the second edition of Ritson's *Robin Hood*, as collated by Sir Frederic Madden." It is conjectured to be "possibly as old as the reign of Edward II." That the murder of a monk should be pardoned in the facile way described is manifestly improbable. Even in the lawless Galloway of 1508, McGhie of Phumpton was fined six merks for " throwing William Schankis, monk, from his horse." (*History of Dumfries and Galloway*, by Sir Herbert Maxwell, p. 155.)

ROBIN HOOD AND THE POTTER.—p. 209.

Published by Ritson, from a Cambridge MS., probably of the reign of Henry VII.

ROBIN HOOD AND THE BUTCHER.—p. 221.

Published by Ritson, from a Black Letter copy in the collection of Anthony Wood, the Oxford antiquary.

www.ingramcontent.com/pod-product-compliance
Lightning Source LLC
Chambersburg PA
CBHW032005230426
43672CB00010B/2253